Excellent Educational Advantages

WAKE FOREST ON CAPITAL-TO-CAPITAL HIGHWAY

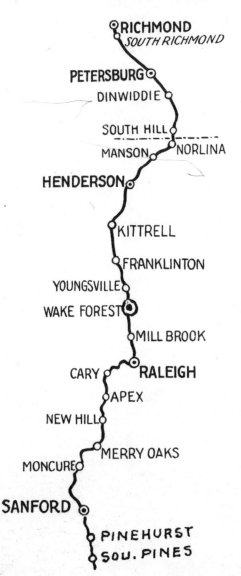

RICHMOND
SOUTH RICHMOND
PETERSBURG
DINWIDDIE
SOUTH HILL
MANSON — NORLINA
HENDERSON
KITTRELL
FRANKLINTON
YOUNGSVILLE
WAKE FOREST
MILL BROOK
CARY — RALEIGH
APEX
NEW HILL
MERRY OAKS
MONCURE
SANFORD
PINEHURST
SOU. PINES

26

CAPITAL PRINTING CO., RALEIGH

"Build in Wake Forest"

WAKE FOREST
NORTH CAROLINA

Invites
Good Citizens

A Good Place In Which to Live

North Main Street

Write Secretary Community Club

CONNECTIONS...
100 Years of Wake Forest History

by Carol W. Pelosi

Top image: 1909 view of the Wake Forest College campus taken from the railroad tracks before the street was lowered and the railroad underpass was constructed. *Courtesy of the Wake Forest College Birthplace Museum*

Bottom image: 2008 view of the Southeastern Baptist Seminary Campus taken from a similar location. *Photograph by Sol Levine*

The Donning Company Publishers
184 Business Park Drive, Suite 206
Virginia Beach, VA 23462

Steve Mull, General Manager
Barbara Buchanan, Office Manager
Wendy Nelson, Editor
Amanda D. Guilmain, Graphic Designer
Derek Eley, Imaging Artist
Lori Kennedy, Project Research Coordinator
Tonya Hannink, Marketing Coordinator
Bernie Walton, Project Director

COVER and TITLE PAGE: Agriculture, education, and the railroad shaped the early years of the village that grew up in the Forest of Wake just north of Forestville, but it was electricity that gave the homes and businesses clustered around Wake Forest College a separate identity as the Town of Wake Forest, chartered in 1909. In the 1909 photograph that inspired this painting, newly installed electric power poles line White Street in Wake Forest's business district. *Artist: Bonnie Brooks*

SEAL, BACK COVER: Original drawing for the Seal of the Town of Wake Forest. *Artist: Theldious Mitchell*

ENDSHEETS: A 1926 brochure compiled and distributed by the Community Club. *Courtesy of the Wake Forest College Birthplace Museum*

Library of Congress Cataloging-in-Publication Data

Pelosi, Carol W.
Connections-- 100 years of Wake Forest history / by Carol W. Pelosi.
    p. cm.
Includes index.
ISBN 978-1-57864-525-1 (hard cover : alk paper)
1. Wake Forest (N.C.)--History. 2. Wake Forest (N.C.)--Social life and customs. 3. Community life--North Carolina--Wake Forest--History. 4. Wake Forest (N.C.)--Biography. I. Title.
F264.W17P45 2008
975.6'55--dc22
                                  2008034715

Printed in the United States of America
at Walsworth Publishing Company

DEDICATION

CONNECTIONS is dedicated to the people of Wake Forest; the real connections who make this the wonderful place it is.

To do justice to the history and richness of life in Wake Forest over a period of 100 years would take an encyclopedia. We could only scratch the surface in this space, attempting to trace the events that shaped the current landscape and capture moments that represent the spirit of our community.

There are so many people, places, and things of tremendous importance that it was not possible to include them all in these pages. We are grateful to those of you who shared your personal pictures and stories. We ask for forgiveness from those of you who feel that we left out images or memories you cherish.

We are grateful, too, to the artists and photographers who so generously donated their work for this publication and to the organizations that shared their archives. In addition, we would like to thank Amy Sawyer, North Carolina Division of State Historic Sites, for enhancing images throughout this book.

We hope that the text and pictures here, as well as the year of Centennial events, bring back happy memories for longtime residents, give newcomers a sense of the past, and create a firm foundation for good conversation and shared experiences for all of us.

The *CONNECTIONS* Committee

The Austin Creek Greenway is part of the town's open space and greenway plan adopted in 2002. *Photograph by Hugh Nourse*

CONNECTIONS...
100 Years of Wake Forest History

TABLE OF CONTENTS

Wake Forest

Equality

Recreation

Education

Religion

1834 · 1951 · 1909

North Carolina

FOREWORD

We are excited to share the history of our community through the pages of this special centennial publication.

Wake Forest enjoys a rich history. As you will learn from this book, our community actually began in the 1800s, but in 1909 our leaders realized that additional services were needed for the residents and they sought and received from the legislature a charter as the Town of Wake Forest.

Over the years our community has grown from a small college town to a community of more than 25,000 residents. As we have grown, our traditions have changed and evolved, yet it is a testament to our people that we have embraced a progressive outlook while retaining our small town charm and appeal.

This publication was written and the pictures assembled entirely by volunteers, showing once again that it is the **people** who make Wake Forest a wonderful place to live.

We hope this publication will jog your memories and serve to introduce you to the people and places that came before us.

As we look forward, we will continue to seek ways to blend the old with the new to maintain the character of our town and the quality of life so cherished by our residents. We are confident that all of the ingredients are in place to ensure the realization of our high expectations for the future.

Mayor Vivian Jones

The Wake Forest College Hospital stood on the college campus at the corner of Durham Road (South Avenue) and Wingate Street.
Postcard courtesy of Frank Drake

preface

When the sun rose on January 1, 1909, three towns were strung along the Seaboard Coast Line tracks in northern Wake County.

Over the course of the next 100 years, the three would become one. How that happened is part of our story along with the lives and the events that shaped the town of today.

On the south was Forestville, the original settlement that had become a thriving commercial center in the early and middle 1800s after the Raleigh & Gaston Railroad built a depot there in 1840. Although it had been incorporated in 1879, it had been slowly losing business and vitality to its neighbor, the Town of Wake Forest College, since 1874, when the college trustees convinced railroad officials to relocate the depot next to the college.

On the north was the Town of Royall Cotton Mills, the newcomer, incorporated in 1907 to allow the mill owners to appoint a constable and fend off any thoughts of annexation—and town taxes—on the part of Wake Forest officials.

The Town of Wake Forest College was, as its name implied, very much a creature of the college, but that was changing because of the businesses that had sprung up on the east side of the railroad tracks, businesses that served the farms and farm families in the area as well as the growing town population.

The towns were seeing the first of many changes the 20th century would bring. There were automobiles on the dirt roads; Wilbur and Orville Wright had proven men could fly.

But when the sun set that winter day, the residents were

Mr. and Mrs. Priestley H. Mangum III
and their daughters, Mary and
Harriette, lived at Greenfields, one
of the large farms near Wake Forest.
Courtesy of Mrs. Turner Ray

The main road from Raleigh to Wake Forest ran through the village of Forestville. The all-important train tracks ran behind this house that fronted on Powell Road.
Courtesy of John and Carol Pelosi

back in all the earlier dark centuries, relying on dirty and dangerous coal-oil lamps and candles for light in homes, in businesses, in the college classrooms and offices, and in the few dormitories the college provided—the fourth floor of Old Main, a few rooms in the 1906 Alumni Building.

The college trustees and faculty and the town's officials—often the same men—wanted lights and electricity, and they had set about getting those the year before. Newspapers had told them how electric bulbs covered a ball that descended in Times Square for the first time as 1908 began. Many of them had traveled to Chicago in 1893 to see the White City, the Columbian Exposition and Fair, where thousands of electric bulbs strung everywhere turned the white buildings into a fairyland at night.

On February 20, 1909, the General Assembly acted on the officials' requests, re-chartering the town as the Town of Wake Forest and giving it the authority to issue bonds for an electric plant.

The town board met for the first time on March 1 and basically continued business as usual although three new commissioners—Charles E. Brewer, C. E. Gill, and F. W. Dickson—were sworn in. They and Mayor Sol J. Allen and Commissioners Z. V. Peed and O. K. Holding adopted all the old ordinances and re-named W. W. Bobbitt as the town policeman with a salary of $35 a month. The only other town employee, not named, was the weigher of cotton.

Bobbitt took a census and found 1,225 people, while Gill later reported the tax value of the property in town was $34,500. The U.S. Census found 1,443 people in town in 1910.

An election on the question of issuing bonds worth $15,000 to build an electric plant was held on April 12, 1909. Of the 109 registered voters, all white males who had paid their poll tax, 88 voted for the bonds and one voted against.

The town commissioners hired B. Parker Rucker of Charlotte to build the plant, advertised $12,000 worth of bonds for 30 years at 6 percent, bought $5,494 of equipment including a Westinghouse generator, and agreed to build a railroad spur cooperatively with Moses Fort, who wanted the spur for his planing mill. Much or all of the generator fuel in the early years was sawdust from Fort's mill.

They purchased a lot on Elm Street for $750 and agreed to add a mayor's office and lock-up to the brick electric light plant.

The electric system began operating the night of November 11, 1909, as *The News & Observer* reported the next day: "There was great cheering by the students when the lights were turned on and they had an informal celebration tonight. There are 17 large tungsten lights on the streets of the town."

An electric light plant was built on Elm Street on a lot purchased from S. W. Brewer and his wife for $750. You can still see the faint words "Water" "Light" on the front. *Courtesy of the Wake Forest College Birthplace Museum*

The rates were simple. If you had two lights and did not use more than 754 kilowatts, you paid $1.25 each month.

Although the college put wiring and electric lights in its dormitories and classrooms, most people adopted the new technology slowly.

> *Dr. I. Beverly Lake Sr., born in 1906, said it was 1915 when his family first had electricity. That was when his father, physics professor J. L. Lake, moved the family from the corner of Pine and College into the house on Faculty Avenue built by the Vann family around 1890. And it was only a few bulbs for light for several years. Lake said he was grown before his mother had a refrigerator. Before that, Mr. Penny brought a cake of ice every morning from the ice plant downtown.*

Police Officer Bobbitt maintained the large tungsten lights, and he was instructed to turn them off when the moon was full because people could see well enough by the moonlight.

1

1910–1919

Before we see how the town and its people looked in 1910, we need to talk about its character, because character was what set Wake Forest apart, making people remember it with respect and love 50 and 60 years later.

The Forest District or the Forest of Wake had been known as an area of refinement and education since the early 1800s. Its residents supported several private schools which drew students from all over Wake County and surrounding counties. But it was the college and the college family that truly solidified the area's reputation. The faculty was known for the breadth of its knowledge and the depth of its religious convictions.

In 1985, Dr. I. Beverly Lake Sr. told the Wake Forest Garden Club members that there were "giants strolling our village sidewalks in my childhood." Those had to include William Bailey Royall, who walked home from Appomattox and joined his father in reconstituting the college, where he was to teach Greek for 62 years. Another "giant" was the college president in 1910, Dr. William L. Poteat.

Doctor Billy, as he was affectionately known, was not only a noted biology professor who introduced the laboratory method to the South, the college president from 1905 to 1927 and a proponent of evolution, but he had ideas about race that were considered progressive in his time. He was likely one of the professors who helped educate Allen Young, the son of local slaves. After Young graduated from Kittrell College and Shaw and taught for some years, he returned to his

Royall Cotton Mill, the town's first industry, was located just north of Wake Forest College. The brick mill building, shown, was renovated in the 1990s and converted into apartments.

hometown to start a private school for black students. Poteat helped him find a place for the first classes in a vacant bedspring factory at the corner of North White and Spring streets. The school became the Wake Forest Normal and Industrial School, where Young was still teaching youngsters up through the 1960s.

At its height, Young's school covered several blocks on the south side of the segregated area of town where former slaves and their families had settled, buying land and building homes. Each morning, men and women left the section to work as maids and yardmen in the Faculty Avenue (now North Main Street) homes and in the smaller homes all over town. They also worked in the freight station on White Street and as laborers at the college, in the stores, offices, and industries in town—the foundries, cotton gins, abattoirs, lumber mills, and blacksmith shops. Young's was the only school for black children when it opened.

The Lake children and other white children attended school in an L-shaped building that still stands at the corner of West Pine Avenue and North Wingate Street. The area and the school were referred to as "Sky Hill," Grady Patterson Jr. said, "My father told me it was called that because in his day as a student at the college a great number of ministerial students lived in the area and the other students referred to them as "sky pilots."

Before the school on South Main Street was built, local white children attended several small schools in the village. Sky Hill, at the corner of what are now West Pine and North Wingate streets, was a three-room school that served much of the town.
Photograph by Sol Levine

What did the town and its people look like?

This decade saw a number of changes, none more radical than in women's clothing. In 1910, women's dresses reached from the neck to the floor, topped by elaborate hats. By 1915, people were talking about "flappers," and in 1925 modish frocks for many touched the knee. In conservative, Baptist Wake Forest, it is unlikely many wore the shorter dresses, but they knew about them.

It was very much a college town, centered on the campus, enlivened by the exuberance of the young male students and the new collegiate baseball and basketball games. There were already rivalries in basketball between Wake Forest and Trinity College (Duke University) and North Carolina A & M (North Carolina State). Football had been discontinued in 1895, but it was revived later without college support, and in 1910 the team members and alumni, not the college, were buying the football equipment.

Baseball was the premier sport, played on the ball field where the Calvin Jones House now stands on North Main Street. Since its beginning on April 16, 1900, when the N.C. A & M Farmers beat the Wake Forest Deacons one to nothing, the Easter Monday game between the two schools had become a tradition, though it would not be until 1935 when the day was made an official state holiday to allow the state legislators to attend with easy consciences.

The three original college buildings built in the late 1830s with bricks made of locally dug clay were still standing: Old Main on the campus, the South Brick House on South Avenue, and the North Brick House on North Avenue, twin sentinels at the ends of Front Street. That was matched by Back Street, now Wingate, where Dr. Calvin Jones' old plantation house had been moved from the site of Old Main and turned into a boarding house.

It was a deeply religious community where life centered on the home, the family, and the church. For the college community and most of the business community, that church was Wake Forest Baptist, organized on August 30, 1835, with 17 members. It was a mostly student congregation at first, meeting in various college buildings. Slowly, then increasingly after the rift at Forestville Baptist Church over the depot's move, the church gained members from the faculty and town. Finally, in 1915, a church building on a corner of the college campus was completed and remains the most beautiful church in the county.

Olive Branch Baptist Church was organized with the help of students and faculty members in 1865 and remained on the college campus until 1879 when the trustees bought the present site on East Juniper Avenue.

Spring Street United Presbyterian Church was organized in 1905 by Allen Young

In 1910, Wake Forest College fielded teams in football, basketball, and baseball. Here, Eugene Daniels poses in his baseball uniform on the college athletic field, which was located where the Calvin Jones House is now. *Courtesy of the Wake Forest College Birthplace Museum*

and others, and its history written in 1980 says, "For the first six months, meetings were held in the old bed spring factory on White Street next to the cotton gin site."

In the mill village was Glen Royal Baptist Church. In 1909, members were meeting in the one-room school building on the site of the present church.

Forestville had both the Forestville Baptist Church, built in 1860, and a church that began sometime between 1845 and 1865 when slaves began to worship secretly under a bush arbor. Some slaves were allowed to attend the services in the Forestville church, sitting in the slave gallery. During a revival in 1866, "Uncle" Nelson Ligon was so moved by the spirit that he jumped from the gallery into the white congregation seated below. That led to the founding of Friendship Chapel Baptist Church.

To the west of town, all local Protestant congregations were to have shared Wake Union Church where there were still the original separate doors for men and women. By 1909, only a Baptist and an Episcopal congregation used the church.

Priestley and Zua Davis and their daughters moved back to Wake Forest from Atlanta in the summer of 1915, and he opened a furniture store on South White Street. One of the couple's first decisions was where to go to church.

"Wake Forest has only one church—the Baptist church—which is the center of all activities," Zua wrote to a friend in Atlanta. "Priestley's father [George Washington Davis, a Confederate veteran and former member of the North Carolina General Assembly] is the clerk of the old Episcopal church about two miles from here. Prior to Grand Papa Davis becoming clerk, my grandfather, Calvin Mitchell, was clerk until he died. We feel it will be best for the children to go to the local church. Grand Papa Davis is not happy about our choice."

Forestville Baptist Church was built in 1860 at a cost of $2,100. Inside, the balcony, which still exists, served as the slave gallery. Members of the church helped formally organize Friendship Chapel Baptist Church after 1866.
Photographs by Sol Levine

WAKE FOREST BAPTIST CHURCH, WAKE FOREST, N. C.

A later letter underlined the closeness of the community. "Everyone attends all school functions and Miss Emma Poteat, the wife of President Billy Poteat, sends a critique of the performance by her maid the next morning."

Wake Forest Baptist Church was first organized on the Wake Forest College campus in 1835 following a student revival. The church building was completed in 1915 at a total cost of $70,000 including organ and stained glass. The round window in the top of the dome is pictured here. *Postcard courtesy of Frank Drake; photograph by Sol Levine*

Faculty Avenue was a wide dirt street graced by many of the houses we admire today, including the William C. Powell house. He, with Thomas E. Holding and Robert E. Royall, all Wake Forest College graduates and brothers-in-law—Powell and Holding married two of Royall's sisters—built the Royall Cotton Mill. Two of Powell's sons, William R. Powell and Robert Powell, would soon build houses beside their father's. Holding had built his Queen Anne home on South Avenue in 1899, and Royall built a different Queen Anne on Faculty Avenue in 1900.

Many of the people living on Faculty Avenue and in houses all over town rented rooms to one, two, or more students, and at least two of the Faculty Avenue houses had been built as boarding houses, renting rooms and selling meals, because the college had little dormitory space and did not provide meals.

Horses, mules, cows, pigs, and chickens were everywhere in town. One of the signature town photographs is a composite panoramic view of the campus showing the arch at the intersection of Wait Avenue. A wagon, the driver, and the mule were captured at the intersection as well as a cow grazing along the street edge. It would be several years before local dairies would deliver milk daily or make it available in stores.

Many homes had a backyard such as few would recognize today, including an outhouse or privy along with a barn for the cow, the horse or mule, the buggy or

Five of the seven children of Walter and Ida Cole, all born on Mill Street in the Royall Mill village, are pictured in this 1918 photograph. Alice, seated, is holding Minnie Lee. Standing are John B., Mary, and Marlon. The other two children were Ervin, who was killed in World War II, and Estelle. Both parents worked in the mill and their children left school when they turned 12 and went to work there as well. Marlon, Minnie Lee, and Estelle still share the house the family bought when the mill began selling the houses to the workers in the 1940s.
Courtesy of the Cole Family

wagon, some chickens, and sometimes a pig or two. Men like Uncle Joe who worked at the Davis house or Uncle Genatus Dent at the J. L. Lake house tended the gardens. Grady Patterson remembers that his Grandfather Lake's large yard held a vegetable garden, an asparagus bed, a strawberry bed, fruit trees, and grapevines.

Inside, most homes had at least one female servant as well as a washerwoman. Zua Davis had Aunt Chloe for a washerwoman for a load that included 14 dresses each week for each of the three girls—a morning dress plus a fresh dress in the afternoon for a drive with Grand Papa Davis. The children's nurse was Senara, Aunt Sarah did the cooking, and Susy did the cleaning.

Travel in 1910 was either by train, in a wagon or buggy behind a horse or a mule, or on foot, and the roads were unpaved, often little more than red clay mud or ruts. Anyone coming north from Raleigh had to travel on Powell Road (Jesse Powell built the first bridge over the Neuse River) through Forestville and up to the campus. There had been at least one road through the campus, but you could not travel north out of town on Faculty Avenue because it ended at a steep bluff near the cotton mill. To go north, a traveler had to turn right onto South Avenue, left onto Front Street, and right again onto Wait Avenue to cross the railroad tracks between the two stations and the Powers Drug Store. Then there was another left turn to follow the dusty track north to Youngsville.

The two railroad stations faced each other across the tracks. The freight station where the weigher of cotton assured that each bale shipped met the standard weight was between the tracks and White Street, and the passenger station was between the tracks and Front Street, facing the college campus.

Cotton was the cash crop in the area, and the one cotton gin site identified in town stood on White Street about where the new CVS stands now. It was owned by C. E. (Cleophas Elvius) Gill, known around town as Mr. Bud, who lived with his sister and three brothers in the South Brick House.

Most of the town's businesses were on and near White Street, including some that would remain in business for decades, through generations of the same family.

The brick building still stands on the east side of the railroad tracks, facing Wait Avenue, that in 1910 was a drugstore operated by Bruce Powers, who had taken over the business in 1908 from his father, Dr. John Benjamin Powers. Dr. Powers originally went into the drugstore business with Thomas Holding, but the partnership was later dissolved.

Holding moved into a two-story frame building a bit farther south and opened his drugstore. His son, T. E. Holding Jr., took over the store in 1915 while his father ran the Bank of Wake on the opposite corner of Jones and White near one of several public wells the town maintained.

In 1890, W. W. Holding had opened a store on White Street, selling groceries, cotton seed, fertilizer, and general merchandise, but his real interest was in cotton. He began to specialize, buying ginned and baled cotton from farmers, grading it and reselling it to the Royall Cotton Mill, the Sterling Cotton Mill in Franklinton, and other area mills.

Another longtime White Street business was Jones Hardware, begun in 1906 by Ira Otis Jones. He and his wife, the former Elizabeth Freeman, lived in the Queen Anne house on South Main Street that her father had built them as a wedding present.

Frank Keith began his own grocery store on White Street in 1913 after working in two other grocery stores, those owned by L. T. Wilson and S. W. Brewer Sr.

The S.W. Brewer store sold seed, feed, groceries, and other staples for farmers who bought on credit in the spring and paid in full after the crops were in. Brewer opened a second bank, Citizens Bank.

The George Bolus Department Store opened about 1917 on the east side of White Street and moved about 10 years later across the street to a double store: men's clothing on the left, women's on the right.

Elizabeth Seawell, born in 1911, grew up at Oakforest, a large plantation near Wake Forest that dates back to a pre-Revolutionary War land grant. Oakforest is one of the rare local homes that has stayed in the same family from the time it was built to the present.
Artist: Mary Benejam

Mary Thomas Bolus, the daughter of a Lebanese family that had moved to Raleigh, married George in 1908 and insisted they make their home in Wake Forest because "it had a better future since it already had Wake Forest College, a cotton mill, a good community and nearby were Youngsville, Rolesville and Falls of the Neuse."

The family made many contributions to the town, but one was critical. During the 1960s, when the town was struggling to overcome the loss of the college, it needed a new source of water and the best choice was to dam Smith Creek on the east side of town. Mary Bolus owned the land along the creek that would be covered by the reservoir. Friends advised her she should be paid but she refused and gave the land for the reservoir to the town.

Mary and George Bolus were the first Catholics in town and held services in their living room for many years. In the 1930s and 1940s, as more Catholics, mostly students, moved to town, a railroad car called St. Peter was parked on a Seaboard siding. It had all the facilities for a small church as well as a bedroom and kitchen for the priest.

Throughout the decade, the town fathers struggled with health problems—malaria and typhoid fever were real threats—and with where to park all the wagons and mules when farmers and their families came to town on Saturday to shop, how to stop people from keeping pigs in their backyards (cows were allowed), and with questions about the electric plant. In 1915, Carolina Power and Light (CP&L) finally won a franchise to provide power to the town, and the town agreed to extend a line to Forestville "provided there are as many as five customers and it is done at no cost to the town." A. M. Harris paid for the installation, $263.50, and was repaid by the customers.

The town fathers turned down H. E. Joyner's (Shorty's father) request for a reduced rate for the current to run his motion picture show.

Robert and Genoa Freeman built this house for their daughter, Elizabeth, when she married Ira Otis Jones in 1903. The artist has shown the house as it was originally built. *Artist: Lynn Conley*

In 1915, the Town of Forestville surrendered its charter although it retained much of its character up through the 1980s, when it was annexed.

In 1917, the United States finally entered what is now called World War I, and President Woodrow Wilson, who had formerly detested and opposed war, threw himself and the entire nation into the effort with a passion. He demanded that "the spirit of ruthless brutality…enter into the very fiber of national life." All sorts of materials were rationed, the American Protective League looked for traitors and sedition in every closet, newspapers and magazines were censored, and the country turned to the American Red Cross for support and womanpower.

Without a local newspaper to record life in the town at the time, it is difficult to recreate those days, but we know almost a third of the nation of 105 million people supported the Red Cross and eight million people, most of them women, labored in the local chapters to produce goods of all kinds, from sweaters and bandages to furniture. Since the Red Cross was active in Wake Forest in later years, it is almost certain women here worked as hard as their sisters across the nation.

The town board minutes do show that in the fall of 1917 the commissioners banned the use of electricity on Mondays to save fuel.

In May of 1918, Secretary of War Newton Baker wrote to the heads of all colleges and schools where 100 or more students were enrolled, telling them that all students would be given military instruction by Army officers and all students 18 and older would be encouraged to enlist. By August, colleges were informed that all students under 21 would be mobilized in less than a year.

On September 14, 1918, the greatest plague the world has seen arrived in Wake Forest as students were registering for classes. First one, then several students fell ill with the Spanish flu.

By the end of that day, sick students filled the beds in the College Hospital, which stood on campus in the northeast corner of South Avenue (N.C. 98) and Wingate, and college officials had to commandeer the Euzelian (debating society) dormitory in Old Main to house even more of the sick. In all, 60 percent of the students and eight

Dr. William Royall built this two-story house in 1875 and lived here until his death in the late 1920s, when it was acquired by the T. E. Holding Jr. family. Local lore has it that the wide front walk was built so that Tom Holding could call his wife when he left the drugstore downtown with the day's receipts, and she would turn on the porch light and wait for him to drive right up to the front steps.

Artist: Judith Pixton

faculty members fell ill that September; six students developed pneumonia and one died. Their nurses were mainly the staff from the School of Medicine.

We do not know how many townspeople became ill or succumbed to the Spanish flu. In Dr. George W. Paschal's *History of Wake Forest College,* he only noted that many died. The town board minutes tell us that one of those was Commissioner R. H. Mitchell, and his replacement on the board, I. O. Jones, was asked to purchase a tent that could be used for all the funerals in the town cemetery. It was about this time that the town board set the boundaries between the black and white sections of the cemetery, and it was at least 80 years before that fence would be removed.

On October 5, hoping to stem the spread of the illness, the town board banned all public meetings and events: the moving picture shows, public schools, churches, and classes at the college. Later, on January 29, 1919, they placed a strict quarantine on the Henry Stallings home. Family members were forbidden to leave the house and others were not allowed to enter.

Typhoid was also rampant at that time, and there were suggestions for a sewer system, but the town board was more interested in a water system. Late in 1919, the white male voters approved $100,000 in bonds for a water system.

Before work on that began, a second round of the Spanish flu attacked people in town, and on February 7, 1920, all public meetings were again banned, but this time college classes and Anniversary Day exercises were allowed to continue as usual.

Two of Dr. Charles Taylor's daughters relax on the porch of their home on Faculty Avenue in the early 1900s (now North Main Street). The house was originally owned by Samuel Wait, the first president of Wake Forest College, and was occupied by the Taylor family—Dr. Charles Taylor was also a college president—until Frank and Carol Smith bought it in 1969.
Artist: Trish Nardozzi

MINNIE RUTH BROWN
APRIL 1915
JUNE 1917

This monument in the Wake Forest Cemetery is a sad reminder of the diseases that took the lives of so many young children in the early part of the century. *Photograph by Karen Evans*

Benjamin Thomas Hicks

In these early years of the 20th century, Benjamin Thomas Hicks was building the houses for the cotton mill's "operatives." Each four-room house with four interior fireplaces housed two families. He probably also built the school for the mill children in 1907, just as he helped build several of the homes along Faculty Avenue.

In the 1930s, remembered as a very old man, he was the lead carpenter for the several barns and buildings, including the massive dairy barn, at John Sprunt Hill's 1,750-acre showplace farm on Falls of the Neuse Road. At the time it was called Forest Hill Farm and later, in 1939 or 1940, the name was changed to Wakefield Farm.

Ed Osborne said his grandfather, S. O. Rich, the farm manager, designed the huge barn. In the mornings Rich would sit with Hicks, the two would consult, draw something on a piece of wood, and then Hicks would build it.

Hicks' family says the Wake Forest Baptist Church builders ran into some major problems when they were constructing the large dome. They turned to Tom Hicks, who made a few drawings on a piece of wood to show them how to construct it and solved their problems.

Hicks learned his trade from his father, who made fine furniture, was a blacksmith, and also made wheels for carts and wagons for the Confederate Army during the Civil War.

Hicks married five times and fathered nine children; at least three wives died in childbirth.

As Hicks grew older, his hearing diminished, but he still worked at Forest Hill Farm, and the week that ended July 9, 1938, he earned $4. On July 15, 1938, he was walking on the railroad tracks near the cemetery crossing (probably the extension of Walnut Avenue) and, as the story goes, he was watching three or four low-flying airplanes, the most modern means of transportation at the time. He did not hear a train approaching. He was struck and killed by Seaboard train Number 19.

Several of his children and grandchildren lived in the mill village, and in 2007 those grandchildren and the entire mill community celebrated their life there, where everyone was part of the mill family.

Benjamin Thomas Hicks. *Courtesy of Roy and Donna Lynam*
Inset: Wakefield Farm barn. *Photograph by Rusty Forrest*

2
1920–1929

In 1920, Mayor John G. Mills Sr. and the town board began a series of improvements that would improve life for people in town and allow growth for more than 40 years.

First, the 1919 water system bonds were increased to $125,000 to include a sewer system. It was a sewer collection system only, because the town had approval from the state—the letter is still in the book of minutes—to release untreated waste into the Neuse River. They did treat the drinking water piped from a small impoundment on Smith Creek by filtering and chlorinating it in a plant on Elm Avenue across from the electric plant.

Although the commissioners entertained the idea of selling the electric system, even obtaining permission to do so from the General Assembly, they also had a 60-year contract with Carolina Power & Light to provide power. The directors at Royall Cotton Mill donated land at the northern end of town for the substation because the mill was switching to electricity to power its machines.

The town board also established the fire department. Before 1921, when Thomas M. Arrington was named the first chief, firefighting was a volunteer effort that rarely did more than prevent nearby buildings from catching fire. The alternative was to call in the Raleigh Fire Department.

There had been some spectacular fires. On June 30, 1915, the newly built Wake Forest Machinery and Hardware Company burned, perhaps due to arson. A Raleigh fire engine responded, arriving in 35 minutes in a driving rain. "After the pumper exhausts the 3,000-gallon water tank within five minutes, the

In 1920 the town built a water treatment plant and elevated water tank across Elm Street from the electric plant. The building has been extensively remodeled and now serves as a dentist's office.
Photograph by Sol Levine

firemen are forced to watch as flames practically gut the three-story building. They also assist with the bucket brigade, which resumes after the water tank is drained," the Wake Forest Fire Department's online history reports.

That led to the establishment of a fire district in the middle of town in 1917. Then in January of 1920, Old Wingate Place, formerly owned by Wake Forest College President Dr. W. M. Wingate, was destroyed even though students did manage to save almost all the furniture. The college purchased the site in 1927 for $5,500 and built a stone-veneer home for the new president, Francis P. Gaines. It is now the seminary president's home and is called Magnolia Hill.

This hose reel was the first piece of equipment owned by the Wake Forest Fire Department. Firemen Cliff Hall and George Macon pulled it in the 1976 bicentennial parade while Karen Macon, dressed as a clown, waved to the crowd. *Courtesy of* The Wake Weekly

The contract for the water system that was awarded on March 25, 1920, included fire hydrants. J. L. Taylor was the assistant chief, there were 19 volunteer firefighters charged with protecting the town, the college, and the cotton mill, and the fire alarm was a bell on a building just east of White Street. The fire department volunteers were excused from paying the street tax: all men 25 to 50 years of age either had to work on town streets three hours each quarter or pay $3. Later, the poll taxes of $3.50 were also excused for the volunteer firemen.

The first apparatus was a hand-pulled, two-wheeled hose reel with 500 feet of hose stored at the water tank. The reel, lovingly restored, stands behind Station Number 1 on East Elm Avenue.

Even though the town board approved buying an American LaFrance fire truck for $1,650, the first fire truck, according to the department's online history, was an "old Westcott automobile purchased from John Brewer and converted by firefighters into a combination chemical and hose wagon. The top is cut off of the car, a bed is

constructed for hose, a basket is installed to hold chemical tanks, and provisions are made for carrying ladders."

The town also installed five fire boxes around town so that residents could send in the alarm when they saw flames.

That same year, 1923, a two-story brick schoolhouse for white children was built on South Main Street; later it was called the Benton Building. Fire Chief Arrington was told to make sure the schoolhouse was wired for fire alarms on each floor.

In 1922, the first public school for black children finally opened at Olive Branch Baptist Church on East Juniper Avenue, and in 1926 that grew into what became known as DuBois High School.

Building that first school was a true labor of love. The Simmons family gave the land. To build the plans drawn up at the Tuskegee Institute, which called for plaster walls painted in pastel colors, large windows, sturdy hardwood floors, wood stoves, and a brick exterior, the community had to raise $1,100 to receive $1,800 from the Julius Rosenwald Fund. Joseph Massenburg, Willie Johnson, and Caleb Winston organized the local effort to raise the money for what was then called the Wake Forest Graded Colored School.

Earlier, in 1921, the town board ordered Home Telephone and Telegraph Company to make sure there were operators on duty 24 hours a day who would give

The first Wake Forest School building housed grades one through 11 and was later called the Benton Building for a school superintendent. It was a part of Wake Forest Elementary School until it was demolished in 1991 to make room for a one-story structure. *Courtesy of the Wake Forest College Birthplace Museum*

"instant notice" to each firefighter when alarms were reported. This means, of course, that Home Telephone had been in town for some years. It is likely it began sometime after 1910, maybe earlier. The date is forgotten. We do know the names of three early operators—Ruby Reid, Marie Joyner, and Cora Shearon—and that their office was in the basement of the T. E. Holding Drug Store.

In the 1920s, Zua Davis wrote to a friend, "I continue forgetting to tell you of our telephone system here. You will laugh, but it's really quite nice in uniting the town by keeping everyone informed. Miss Ruby Reid is the operator. She listens to all the calls, and if the girls call and I'm not at home, she tells them where I am. There are no secrets in Wake Forest."

Ruby Reid went on to become an astute businesswoman, selling insurance from her home on South White Street, a two-story white house with a picket fence where the Hale Building and its parking lot now stand. She never married, and in her will she left money for a child-care center that became the Ruby Reid Child Care Center on Wingate across from the seminary. It has since moved to Capcom Avenue.

Marie Joyner came to Wake Forest after she was hired as an operator by Home Telephone. She later married "Shorty" Joyner and continued to work, playing the piano at the silent movies and working at the B&S Department Store, where she also played Santa. She was active in many community activities and clubs, and she was famed locally for the decorations she made for the tree at the annual Christmas Tea, all from discarded or recycled items, including sardine cans.

Inquiring minds were not confined to the Home Telephone office. Lawrence Stallings, who would later become famous for "What Price Glory," had been courting Helen Poteat, Dr. Billy and Emma's daughter. He left town to fight in World War I, where he lost a leg, and continued his courtship by letters and postcards. Once he wrote to Helen that he couldn't write more because he knew Miss Annie Crudup, the postmistress, would read it. When he returned to town and went to the post office, Miss Annie said, "Why Lawrence, why did you write that on your card? You know I don't read the cards."

The entrance to the Royall Cotton Mill Commissary after the building was remodeled into apartments in the early 1990s. It was placed on the National Register of Historic Places in 1991. *Artist: Mary Hayes*

The post office had never had a settled home up to this time and would not until 1940. During the 1920s the mail was dispensed—there was no home delivery—from rented space next door to the T. E. Holding Drug Store. Later it moved down the street to a building tucked into a corner of the Forest Theatre.

Voters approved a Recorder's Court (the forerunner of District Court) and it opened in space leased from T. E. Holding.

Crenshaw Hall was one of the large plantations near Wake Forest and, at one time, served as the post office for the college community. The students complained about mail only arriving twice a week by stage and petitioned to have the post office moved to Forestville where mail came daily by train. John Martin Crenshaw was the first student to register in Wake Forest College, but at that time he lived with his parents along Horse Creek in a large house called Waterfall. He moved to Crenshaw Hall after he married his widowed cousin, Louisa Crenshaw Norman. *Courtesy of the Wake Forest Historic Preservation Commission*

One of the most visible improvements was the new national road, U.S. 1. It linked towns all along the eastern seaboard from Maine to Florida. The second was a new state road connecting Wake Forest to Durham, N.C. 98. Both were completed in 1923.

The route for U.S. 1 led to a tremendous wrangle in which the town eventually triumphed over the federal government. The original Wake Forest-Youngsville road was on the east side of the railroad tracks (North White Street now), but the federal engineers chose to lay out the new highway on the west side and in doing so had to tame the steep bluff at the north end of Faculty Avenue.

The federal engineers wanted the new road to continue down Faculty Avenue, straight through the campus, and down what is now South Main, heading for Raleigh.

The town fathers and the college officials said no. It was true a road had gone through the middle of campus once, but that was years past. Finally, the engineers acquiesced and the highway swept around the campus.

If you have paved roads and long-distance motorists, you need gasoline filling stations, and A. J. "Jack" Medlin was happy to oblige, an action that led to the first zoning case heard by the state Supreme Court. He built his general store on Faculty Avenue at the corner of West Juniper Avenue (now the office for Utility Service Agency) in 1905. "I bought my first air rifle there," Dr. I. Beverly Lake Sr. remembered. Medlin installed a dining room in part of the store, and converted his house next door for a tourist lodge. The next step was to enlarge his curbside filling station and put in gasoline pumps.

The thought shook the families in the large Faculty Avenue homes, who apparently believed the pumps and stored gasoline would be a danger to children and the college campus.

They appealed to the town board in December of 1928, which then turned to Wake Forest College President F. P. Gaines and to law Professor R. L. McMillan. McMillan gave the board "a very instructive and entertaining talk about zoning," and at the same time another law professor, John G. Mills, reported on his conferences with James H. Pou, the top lawyer in the county at the time, and Judge Mouring "in regard to abolishing the filling station."

Mayor Dr. Solomon P. Holding and the commissioners—J. C. Caddell; W. R. Powell, who operated the Royall Mill store and was a director there; G. H. Greason, the mill superintendent; and R. W. Wilkinson, a merchant—waited 20 days before adopting a zoning ordinance with only one provision: it became illegal to maintain or operate a gasoline filling station west of the railroad tracks. Zoning was very new, having begun in New York City in 1925 and in Durham in 1927.

Medlin cooperated by operating the station until he was charged, taken to court, and fined $50. He then appealed to the North Carolina Supreme Court, and the case

This photograph from the 1920s shows more than a thousand pounds of baled dried salmon—used to feed the Crenshaw Hall dogs during the winter—and salmon drying on the barn for household use. The children had probably been working under the supervision of W. Martin Jones. *Information and photograph courtesy of the Wake Forest Historic Preservation Commission*

A general store and filling station on North Main, now the office for Utility Service Agency, led to the first zoning case heard by the state's Supreme Court when, in 1929, the town adopted an ordinance prohibiting the sale of gasoline west of the railroad.
Artist: Lynn Conley

was heard in the spring of 1930. Medlin lost, but by then he had the support of many town residents. Mayor Holding, remembered by the park the town built on the site of his South Main home, said the store was "the nicest in town." Dr. George W. Paschal spoke for Medlin as did Dr. Needham Y. Gulley, the dean of the law school and owner of Forestville Dairy. Gulley said his home "is the nearest residence on the east side of Main Street to Mr. Medlin's place of business. I live just across the pasture from Mr. John Mills." The case is a landmark in the state because it upheld the validity of zoning.

No one apparently ever objected to Medlin's tourist home or to the others on North and South Main streets that would flaunt neon signs for years.

Many streets were paved in addition to North and South Main. In 1924, the voters approved $110,000 to pave some unspecified streets—the town board minutes in longhand were casual, often indecipherable, and sometimes the page was blank except for the meeting date—and shortly afterward voters approved another $65,000 to pave Jones, White, and Wait.

It is important to note that the town board met in secret during those days. People could and did appear to speak about issues, but they had to leave before the mayor and commissioners deliberated. The board's decisions were posted on a public notice board. Also, the town board could and did change the fiscal year to suit the financial needs of the town and at least once set the tax rate before looking at the budget needs.

The same laissez-faire attitude was evident at the cotton mill. "During the years 1921 to 1927, the mill leaked liquid assets like a broken pitcher," Don Johnson Jr. wrote in an unpublished thesis written at Princeton University in 1945. Johnson's father had married into the Powell family and became the mill manager in the 1930s. Dividends of 46 percent were paid to stockholders during those years. The salaries for the mill management, essentially the Powell family members, were as high as $7,500 in an era when full professors at the college were paid $3,300.

There was apparently a much different attitude at the town's longest-lived financial institution, the Wake Forest Building and Loan Association. Still thriving today with the word Savings substituted for Building and Federal added to its name, it was chartered on January 5, 1922, with seven members: Samuel Wait Brewer, John M. Brewer, I. O. Jones, W. J. Harper, F. W. Dickson, and F. J. Duke were all merchants, and R. M. Squires was a dentist.

The college was probably in the best financial shape, with an increased endowment and the largest enrollment ever. It also had the Denmark Student Aid Fund, set up to aid needy students and the first student loan fund at a United States college. The fund also became the till into which the mill and the town dipped. The mill's debt to the fund grew to $10,000, a debt that was repaid anonymously many years later, probably by Don Johnston Sr.

The town was making money from the sale of electricity and water—just over $8,000 for electricity and over $4,000 for water in 1931 when it was finally noted in the minutes—but by that year the town's debt was $256,500 with interest amounting to $32,000 each year and a general fund budget of $9,000.

Many sectors of the local economy were feeling pinched. There had been a brief economic recession in 1920 and 1921, and in 1922 cotton dropped to 8 cents a pound from its usual 40 to 50 cents. Farmers could not get enough for their crop at the cotton gin to pay off the debt at the store where they had run up credit during the year. First farmers, then merchants and gin owners, then people all over town were digging in empty pockets.

RESIDENCE OF MAYOR A. J. DAVIS, WAKE FOREST, N. C., COVERED WITH

BIRD'S
NEPONSET
Twins

We recommend NEPONSET Twin Shingles for fine residences and comfortable homes because they are artistic and waterproof, quick and easy to lay, and approved by the National Board of Fire Underwriters.

Manufactured by
BIRD & SON, inc. E. Walpole, Mass.
Established 1795
Chicago Office and Plant, 1472 W. 76th St.
New York Office, 295 Fifth Ave.
Bird & Son, Ltd., Hamilton, Ont.

SOLD BY
WAKE FOREST SUPPLY CO., WAKE FOREST, N. C.
LET US LOOK AFTER YOUR ROOFING NEEDS

8211 5 26 5000 R O 1290

This advertising blotter was given away to customers at Jones Hardware in the 1920s.
Courtesy of Margaret Jones Stinnett

There were cotton gins at almost every four corners in the county, but the gins began to disappear in 1927 when the boll weevil reached Wake County, destroying crops in the field.

The economy began another major shift. In the late 1700s and up through the Civil War, the land in Wake Forest Township had been in large tracts, plantations, held by a few individuals and families who used slave labor. After the war, those were gradually broken into smaller farms where individuals and families labored themselves or with sharecroppers to raise food for themselves and a cash crop of cotton. Once the boll weevil reached the area, an estimated 1,000 farmers in the county shifted to another crop or, overwhelmed by debts, had to sell their land.

The shift was to dairy farming, assisted by improvements in refrigeration and the development of the Pine State Creamery Company in Raleigh in 1919. Soon Wake Forest was encircled by dairy farms, including the 1,000-acre Holding farm just to the southeast, the equally large Marshall dairy (later Marshall-Stroud) on the south, the Esley Forbes farm on the south, the showplace John Sprunt Hill farm to the southwest, and the James Lye farm to the west.

Both dairy and mixed farming existed out in the Harricane area, and to the east, where the land is flatter, tobacco became the cash crop.

In town, the people who lived in the small houses along Jones and Owen, over on North Avenue and College Avenue, and even in the grander homes along North Main were caught up in the financial downward spiral. People began to fall behind on their tax payments and street assessments. In 1929, when the property tax rate was $1.50 per $100 value and the total assessment was $15,000, only a third of that amount was paid.

Wake County held tax sales, auctioning off the property of delinquent taxpayers. The Wake Forest commissioners told their attorney, John G. Mills, to do what he could to protect the town's interests.

The answer was to buy the properties. Mills bought the George Green property for $100, the A.P. Johnson property for $135, and the Vance Sikes property for $25, all in one month. In one year, the town paid $2,379.05 to buy houses and lots, in another the tab was more than $5,000.

Even though they were borrowing to pay the interest on the town debt, the commissioners drew up plans for a fire department building that would cost $1,500 and a municipal and court building for $5,500. The fire department building never became reality, but the municipal and court building—the square gray stucco building at the corner of East Owen Avenue and Brooks Street—was built and now houses most of the town's planning and inspections departments.

Some spring chicks awaited their removal to another home in the window of the Arrington store. *Courtesy of the Arrington Family*

Members of David and Ruby Ray's family barned tobacco in the mid-1950s. If the harvest was later than usual, schools did not open until the tobacco was in. *Courtesy of the Ray Family*

Annie Lowery on Bent Road in 1921.
Courtesy of JoAnn Rogers

Charles Lowery at his Bent Road farm.
Courtesy of JoAnn Rogers

CONNECTIONS ...

Farms & Crops

The Town of Wake Forest was surrounded by farms, large and small. Churches and small stores were scattered through the rural areas, but the children attended Wake Forest schools and downtown merchants depended a great deal on the farmers' trade. There were several large dairies near town; cotton and tobacco were major money crops. Most small farmers raised their own vegetables, chickens, pigs, and feed corn, and nearly everyone had at least one mule for plowing, a horse to pull the wagon, and a milk cow.

Linwood Walters and his wife, Jenny, raised two daughters on their small farm west of Wake Forest. His daughter Theresa Adams remembers that he loved his daughters and grandsons, loved growing stuff, and loved singing gospel at Rock Spring Baptist Church. Walters was born in 1922 and died on Mother's Day in 1996. *Photograph by Simon Kearney*

Tobacco barns once dotted the countryside. Tobacco was picked by hand, tied into bundles on sticks, and the sticks were hung in the barns while the tobacco was cured. In the early days, wood fueled the fires; later most farmers converted to propane. *Artist: Wyn Easton*

3
1930–1939

All during 1930 and 1931, the commissioners worried
that the town's sinking funds—the money for the debt
payments—might not be safe.

At first they kept those funds in the Citizens Bank run by the
Brewer family, who told the town board the funds were personally
guaranteed by the bank's directors. Uneasy, the commissioners
moved the money to T. E. Holding's Bank of Wake shortly before
Citizens Bank closed its doors in late 1929 or early 1930.

Almost every month the commissioners appointed a
committee to make sure the bank had enough collateral to cover
the funds. In December of 1931, Commissioner Percy Wilson
said he and F. W. Dickson "had repeatedly seen the officers of
the Bank of Wake (and)…that the directors of the bank had not
furnished the promised collateral but promised the furnishing of
an adequate bond…that Mr. Harvey Holding was preparing the
bond and would be delivering it to the town as issued."

The Bank of Wake closed its doors on December 17, 1931.
Fortunately for the town, the collateral, consisting of personal
loans, had been issued, and people continued to pay off the debt
up through 1934, when the town finished collecting the entire
amount.

The debts paid included $75 from Pearl Ray, a teacher;
$100 from J. L. Taylor, the chief of police who was elected fire chief
in 1933 replacing Thomas Arrington; $1,000 from W. W. Holding
Jr., a cotton broker and dairy farm owner; and $506.88 from
R. W. Wilkinson Sr., a merchant who built the three-story

The Wilkinson Building, built around 1900, housed R. W. Wilkinson Sr.'s general store, shown here in 1931. The first movie theater in Wake Forest was located on the first floor on the Wait Street side, Chester H. Wilkinson ran a dry-cleaning business in the basement, and college students lived on the second and third floors. Later Dr. R. W. Wilkinson Jr. and Dr. C. T. Wilkinson had offices in the building. *Courtesy of R. W. Wilkinson III*

Wilkinson Building at the corner of South White Street and Wait Avenue and operated a department store there.

> *Zua Davis wrote to her friend in Atlanta, "The Depression has hit…with a vengeance! Dorothy and Margaret [two of her daughters] were on their way to Meredith when they heard that the local bank had closed. I had sold government bonds the day before so they could pay their tuition. They came home to see what to do. I told them to go ahead because everyone is in the same predicament."*
>
> *With her girls in college, Zua rented her upstairs rooms in her South Main house to two professors. "The rent is most helpful in these difficult times." She was later to write that she did get 10 cents on the dollar for her lost savings, but not until much time had passed. Her uncle S. Berry Perry ("Peddy") was president of the Bank of Youngsville which held on until 1933, never reopening after the bank holiday that year. He did eventually repay everyone fully.*

Wake Forest Girl Scouts picnicked at the Golf Pond in 1938. Enjoying the outing are Margaret Johnston, Nancy and Lib Brian, Mary Harris, Helen Sanders, Betty Sue Joyner, Jane Harris, Selma Ann Harris, Alice Lee, Elizabeth Jones, Margaret Carroll, and, standing, Annie Jessup and Betty Stansbury. *Courtesy of the Wake Forest College Birthplace Museum*

Many people lost all their savings. Roy Powell, who was the town clerk for several years, remembered he was in his early teens when the Bank of Wake failed and he lost everything he had in there. Not much, he would admit, but it was a blow.

In May of 1932, the town commissioners petitioned the college to help in the crisis, "owing to the second local bank failure and the long discontinuance of work in industry here," by allowing the 20 young women who had just graduated from high school to enroll at the college for the 1932–1933 school year. The college denied the request.

Then came the fires, and people listened fearfully for the electric siren in downtown that signaled the location of each blaze. Each volunteer fireman—chief, assistant chief, and 27 men—had an alarm in his home.

The first fire was discovered in the early morning hours of May 5, 1933, in Wait Hall, also called Old Main, built in 1837 as the first college building. The small Wake Forest Fire Department knew immediately that the fire was beyond its limited means and called in the Raleigh and Louisburg departments for help. It was in vain. Most of the townspeople and all the students and professors watched the building burn to the ground as the sun rose.

WAKE FOREST HIGH SCHOOL, WAKE FOREST, N. C.

This fine two- and three-story building, still the main building for Wake Forest Elementary, is exactly like the building completed in 1933 that was the second victim of an arsonist. *Postcard courtesy of Frank Drake*

Not even a month later, on May 31, 1933, there was a second major fire. The Wake Forest School District had just completed a fine brick two- and three-story building on West Sycamore to house grades one through 11. Once again the fire began about midnight but was beyond control when it was discovered. "Efforts of local firefighters are futile," the fire department history says. The loss was estimated at $60,000, but the district had insured the building and speedily rebuilt it as first planned. Now named the R. H. Forrest Building after a longtime teacher, principal, and superintendent, it remains the major building for Wake Forest Elementary today.

Arson, people said fearfully. Firemen and ordinary people began to take action.

"My father and other men used to sit up into the wee hours of the dawn with loaded guns to protect their own," Grady Patterson remembers. "In the business district, the W. W. Holding cotton gin made a spectacular blaze one night." He says many structures in town were burned, and "it was believed that a pyromaniac was loose in the town. A number of people who did not experience fires found collections of oily rags and other fire-making materials which it was thought had been left by the miscreant." (One of T. E. Holding's sons then owned the Gill cotton gin. Its last owner was Obie C. Garner.)

The second campus fire destroyed Wingate Hall, which had become the college's oldest building, on February 14, 1934. Six days later, about 3 a.m. on February 20, a wad of burning paper was found stuffed under the floor at the south end of Hunter Dormitory and there was some damage. On March 2, 1934, again in the early morning hours, a fire began in the Wake Forest Golf Club (now Paschal) clubhouse and it burned to the ground.

The Wake Forest College trustees had been reluctant to help the town with fire protection, especially since they had been forced to cut professors' salaries that spring, but after the Wingate Hall fire the trustees agreed to pay half the cost for a pump on a Chevrolet chassis that could pump 400 gallons per minute. The cost was $1,524.68, and the truck was called Maude.

The person or persons responsible was never found, though many suspected a college student who left town after the 1934 spring semester and did not return. There were no more fires after he left.

In 1982, Thomas Arrington Jr., son of the original fire chief and later a fire chief himself, said more than 70 fires were set over the two-year period and 17 buildings were burned. Every building on campus had a fire set in it, though most were found in time to save the building.

Despite the fire losses—which were not just the buildings but also irreplaceable portraits, books, and records—the college was in good financial shape compared to the town and the mill.

Because of the high dividends and high salaries paid to the officers during the 1920s and because northern competition was stressing all the textile mills in the state, Royall Cotton Mill went into receivership (bankruptcy) and was reorganized as Royal Cotton Mill with Don P. Johnston, the son-in-law of one of the mill's founders, W. C. Powell, as president.

The mill workers were desperately poor. In 1931, the highest-paid spinner who worked 55 hours a week took home $7.94. Spoolers working the same hours made between $14.96 and $15.51. Pay scales were lowered as the Depression went on. The mill stopped charging rent for the houses and urged families to grow vegetable gardens and raise pigs.

There was a Local Welfare Committee, but it apparently concerned itself with white townspeople, not mill workers or black families. Mrs. Hubert Poteat and Mrs. Thomas Arrington asked the town board in 1935 to forgive the electric and water bills for one woman. In 1936, the town appropriated $10 for poverty relief.

Money problems struck at all social levels. William R. Powell, W. C. Powell's son, was one of the mill's directors and operated the company store. He built one of the showplaces on North Main Street, called Cameron Heights, and his wife, Susie Cameron Lanneau Powell, founded the Wake Forest Garden Club with her neighbors. They owed back taxes, and in 1934, a year after William resigned from the town board, the commissioners ordered their attorney to proceed with foreclosure or forced sale. The matter was settled a month later when other members of the Powell family transferred some bonds to the town to pay the taxes.

This clay wall hanging is based on an Arrington family picture dated August 1939. The notation on the back reads, "William and Maude destroying 3 A of cotton planted in excess of quota."
Artist: Gail Hancock

T. E. Holding, one of the mill's founders, had died in 1930 before his bank failed. The family nearly lost the Victorian home he built on South Avenue, but the town accepted three lots valued at $5,000 in lieu of the back taxes.

A high tax rate led to a taxpayer mini-revolt in the early 1930s. In 1932, when the rate was $1.25 per $100 valuation, several prominent residents protested and the rate was dropped to $1.15. The next year there was another protest and the rate was dropped to $1. They also protested the high salaries Mayor Andrew J. Davis—$600 a year—and the commissioners were paid.

In 1935, a totally new town board was elected, many of them the men who had protested the tax rate earlier: Mayor S. W. Brewer, a merchant; and Commissioners Harvey Holding, a businessman; Don Johnston, the mill president; Dr. George W. Paschal, professor of Greek; Clyde Coppedge Sr., a businessman; and Dr. C. S. Black, also a college professor. The mayor's salary was cut to $300, and the board began to sell the properties the town had acquired through the tax sales, although they also pressed by every means possible for the payment of all past and current taxes and street assessments.

The town slowly began to get on a sound financial footing, and the rock for its finances was the electric system, which made money every year, even when rates were cut to 8 cents per kilowatt hour. Taxes brought in between $7,500 and $11,000, but the electric system paid back $14,000.

The commissioners also chased every New Deal dollar on the horizon. A grant of $31,090 helped improve the water system. The town put up $2,500 in cash in 1935 and the federal government and the state together spent $11,000 to build a gymnasium at the school on West Sycamore. In 1937, federal dollars helped build Back Street (soon renamed Wingate) from Front Street south to West Sycamore.

There were many accidents involving trains and vehicles through the years, but perhaps the most horrific occurred at the Wait Avenue crossing in 1931 when a train crashed into a school bus, killing two students, John Caddell Jr. and Robert Garner.

The road between the campus and the downtown area in 1932 crossed the railroad tracks just across from the arch. The water tower near Elm Street can be seen behind the trees. *Courtesy of the North Carolina State Archives*

In 1937, the underpass connecting the residential/college area and the downtown was built to comply with federal regulations that rail crossings be grade-separated. The Underpass Grocery was tucked in at street level. *Courtesy of the Pleasants Family*

Because of that accident and others like it across the nation, the federal government began requiring that crossings be grade-separated. In 1937, the underpass was built along with Roosevelt Avenue, and Wait Avenue became a dead-end street at the tracks, although vehicles could cross the tracks to reach the depot parking lot.

> The construction left "a red clay gulch on the east side of the campus to and up past the underpass," I. Beverly Lake Sr. recalled in 1985 in a speech to the Wake Forest Garden Club. "It was a local horror, called the Grand Canyon, and it was the Garden Club who brought about its softening and sodding and the planting along the railroad of the lovely crabapples and forsythia."

The Works Progress Administration (WPA) built the first post office building; all earlier post offices had been either in the postmaster's home or in rented spaces. Completed in 1940, the brick building still stands on South White Street across from The Cotton Company with its original mural now covered by wallpaper.

No one could attend the town commissioners' deliberations, and few people appeared before them to speak. The first instance noted in the minutes of two black men appearing was in January of 1937 when Luther Tuck and Allen Young

The United States Post Office on White Street was built by the Works Progress Administration. *Courtesy of the Wake Forest Chamber of Commerce*

came as representatives of an East End neighborhood council. They asked for street improvements, street lights, police protection, and fire alarm boxes.

As a result, Tuck was appointed a special policeman to be paid from the court fees. Public Works Superintendent Oscar M. McKaughan was told to "investigate the necessity for street lights in the negro section." There was no further mention of street lights in the minutes, but the town did install fire hydrants near the new DuBois School.

The 1930s were a time for consolidation of schools, black and white, from the scattered one- and two-room country schools to larger schools, usually in towns, with more comprehensive programs, though black public schools were still funded at about half the rate of white public schools.

From 1937 through 1941, under the guidance of Principal L. R. Best, the following schools were joined with the Wake Forest DuBois School: Rolesville, Wyatt near Forestville, Genesis Branch west of Wake Forest, Macedonia and St. Mary's near Rolesville, and Ray School on the Durham highway.

In 1939, Wake County built the high school building and the school was renamed DuBois High School with grades eight through 11. The first 12th-grade class was added in 1947.

Hired in the late 1930s, Rosa Holding Winston was the first woman police officer in Wake Forest. *Courtesy of Willis Winston*

Just blocks away, Allen Young's Wake Forest Normal and Industrial School, which began in 1905 and prospered during the 1920s and early 1930s, was dealt a hard blow by the new public high schools. It had been the first high school for black students in Wake County and operated the first school bus for black students in the county. Parents and students, some from as far away as Pennsylvania and Connecticut, had turned to Young's board and day school because there was little or no public schooling for black youth. Young and his teachers—11 of them by the mid-1920s teaching 366 students—set rigorous moral, intellectual, and practical standards for their charges. The school and its buildings along Spring Street and Pine Avenue would continue through the 1960s, but they would be diminished.

In Wake Forest there were local efforts to stimulate the economy and help the town, most notably the Men's Civic Club with Sam Sidenburg, owner of B&S Department Store, as the president. They wanted the town to thrive as "a trading center" and offered a number of recommendations, including paving the block of White Street south of the (rented) post office, procuring a newspaper that would give merchants a way to advertise and would aid civic pride, and the need for a ladies' public restroom for out-of-town shoppers.

When town residents were asked to suggest improvements, those included a sidewalk on each side of Durham Road, a modern post office, city mail delivery, street signs and numbers for houses, prohibiting pigs and dairies inside town, making the business section more attractive by sweeping the streets every morning and keeping the sidewalks clean, signs on the highway showing

the way to the business section, and removal of rubbish on vacant lots.

In the October 16, 1937, edition of *The Old Gold & Black*—the college newspaper was then devoting a page or two to town affairs—there was an article saying Wake Forest voters would decide on November 9 whether three streets would be paved: the one block on South White from the post office down to Elm Street (sic) and the water tank, one block on Elm from the water tank across the railroad tracks to South Main, and West Sycamore from South Main to South Wingate. There was no mention of the size of the bond issue, but it apparently did not pass because the town board minutes later said the town received federal funds to pave those streets and build curbs, gutters, and sidewalks.

The Civic Club was taking credit for the markers—concrete monuments with street names that can be seen in some contemporary photographs—recently placed at intersections in town and for the new names for the streets. The club wanted to improve the business section by moving the telephone poles to the back alleys.

Allen Young's (pictured at left) Wake Forest Normal and Industrial School, a private school for blacks on Spring Street, educated both boarding and local students from 1905 until the 1960s. *March 27, 1956, issue of* The Student *magazine at Wake Forest College, courtesy of the Wake Forest College Birthplace Museum*

U.S. Highway 1 went through the center of Wake Forest and several tourist homes were built along the route. Wooten's Hometel and Restaurant on South Main was the largest and it also had a dining room that served local groups as well as travelers. *Postcard courtesy of John Wooten Jr.*

Another project was either the reconstruction or the removal of the freight station along South White Street. Sidenburg called it "one of the worst eyesores now in use on the Seaboard line" and suggested it could be rebuilt either there or outside of town.

Perhaps it is best to end this decade with a short memoir that reflects how people remember the Wake Forest of their youth.

Grady Patterson was born into the Lake family and lived on Faculty Avenue in the 1930s. In 2007, prompted by a remark about the new bed and breakfast, he wrote: "I believe the bed and breakfast house about which you speak is the two-story house located on the east side of North Main on the corner one block north of the campus.

"During my childhood it belonged to Mr. Reid, who was the stationmaster at the old Seaboard Railroad freight station downtown. In the house immediately south of it, two sisters, Miss Sallie Perry and Mrs. Maude Bowers, operated a boarding house for students. I can remember riding my bike up the street about 5:30 on summer afternoons and watching the student diners gathered on the porch awaiting the supper bell, while the smell of fried chicken filled the air from that house and Miss Jo Williams' boarding house down on the corner, a building recently occupied by The Corner Ice Cream Shop.

Just two doors down from the Hometel was Seven Gables, where Mrs. Frank Parker catered to overnight guests. According to John Wooten, whose father ran the Hometel, she mostly accommodated the overflow. *Postcard courtesy of Frank Drake*

"The Perry-Bowers house later became Magnolia Inn tourist home, one of two in the town of Wake Forest. The other was Mr. Jack Medlin's Shady Oaks Tourist Home a couple of blocks north on the other side of the street. With neon signs out front, they each had a flourishing trade. As you probably know, U.S. 1 ran directly through town on North Main in those days, which meant that anyone driving up or down the East Coast passed through our sleepy little village."

SEVEN GABLES For Over-night Guests
Mrs. J. Frank Parker, Hostess
U. S. No. 1. South Wake Forest, N. C.

We hate to contradict memories, but there were also two tourist homes on South Main Street, the Wooten's Hometel, where civic clubs met in the basement dining room, and Seven Gables, which advertised fried chicken, ice cream, and a separate locked garage. North of town, right on the Franklin County line, was the Wake Forest Inn, which also had cabins.

CHICKEN
and
WAFFLES
or
STEAK
and
POTATOES
50¢

On New Year's Eve in 1937,
Johnny Newsom was prepared
to eat well for 50 cents. *Courtesy
John Wooten Jr.*

WAKE FOREST 342
542·946
NORTH CAROLINA · 37

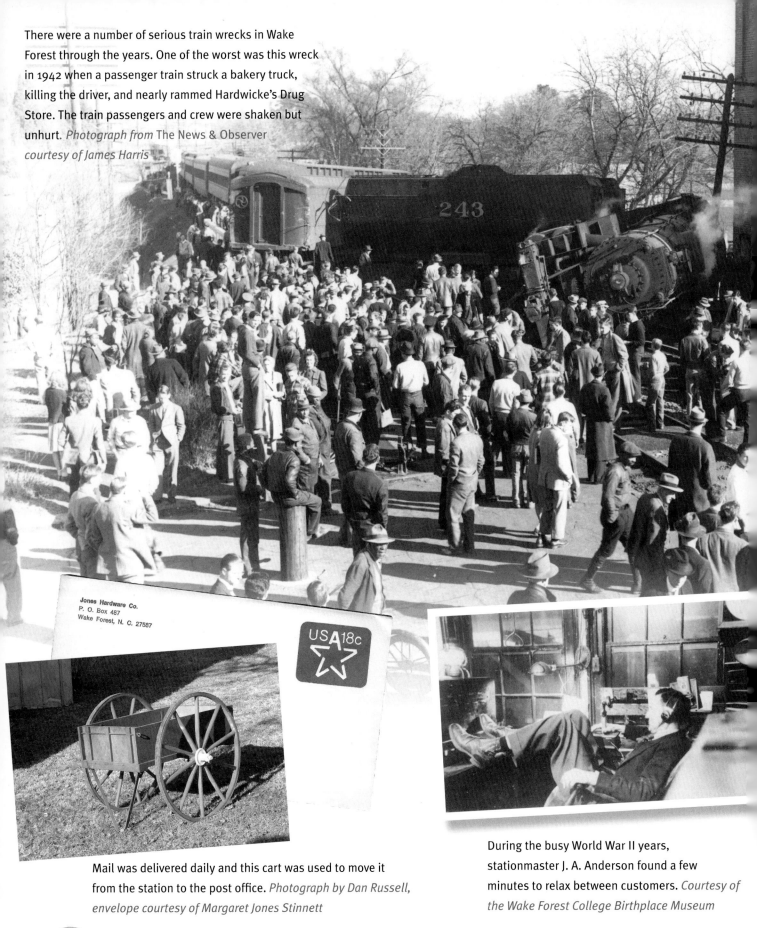

There were a number of serious train wrecks in Wake Forest through the years. One of the worst was this wreck in 1942 when a passenger train struck a bakery truck, killing the driver, and nearly rammed Hardwicke's Drug Store. The train passengers and crew were shaken but unhurt. *Photograph from* The News & Observer *courtesy of James Harris*

Jones Hardware Co.
P. O. Box 487
Wake Forest, N. C. 27587

USA 18c

Mail was delivered daily and this cart was used to move it from the station to the post office. *Photograph by Dan Russell, envelope courtesy of Margaret Jones Stinnett*

During the busy World War II years, stationmaster J. A. Anderson found a few minutes to relax between customers. *Courtesy of the Wake Forest College Birthplace Museum*

CONNECTIONS ...

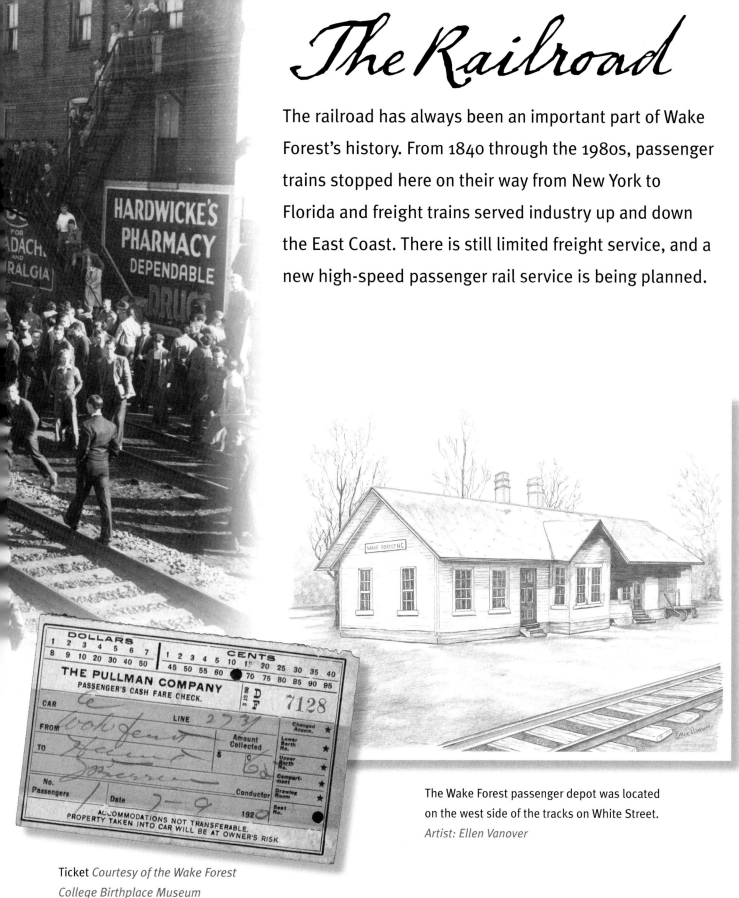

The Railroad

The railroad has always been an important part of Wake Forest's history. From 1840 through the 1980s, passenger trains stopped here on their way from New York to Florida and freight trains served industry up and down the East Coast. There is still limited freight service, and a new high-speed passenger rail service is being planned.

The Wake Forest passenger depot was located on the west side of the tracks on White Street.
Artist: Ellen Vanover

Ticket *Courtesy of the Wake Forest College Birthplace Museum*

4
1940–1949

War was far away in Europe as 1940 began. Of much more interest were the two meetings in February of that year that would change the face of Wake Forest and the countryside around it.

On Groundhog Day, Randolph Benton, the superintendent of the Wake Forest school district, invited E. T. Kearns Jr., the vocational teacher, to speak at a meeting of about 40 local farmers. Kearns told them how farmers in Davidson County and surrounding counties had organized a cooperative and were serving themselves with electricity.

Wake Forest had had electricity for 30 years, but outside the town limits, the barns and homes were dark. Out Purnell and Stony Hill roads, over around Rolesville, people were raising chickens, running dairy farms, and harvesting tobacco entirely by hand. Try pumping enough water for 1,500 chickens day after day. "Everybody was living in poverty except the bootleggers," Worth Pearce, a farmer near Stony Hill, said.

Carolina Power & Light, like other electric utilities across the country, thought farmers would not use enough electricity to justify the cost of building the lines. If a farmer said he wanted a line, he had to pay between $2,000 and $3,000 a mile to get it to his property.

The first spark came from the Rural Electrification Administration created in 1936, but farmers still had to organize a cooperative, build the lines, and find a source for power. In Wake Forest, they had help.

Members of the 1949 Home Demonstration Club prepared to serve refreshments at the Community House. Included in the group are Helen Hollowell, Lily Powell, Allyne Wiggins, Mary Satterwhite, Nellie Hunt, and Ruth Snyder. *Courtesy of the Wake Forest College Birthplace Museum*

The effort had hefty local support. Dr. Thurman Kitchin, Wake Forest College president, was at the meeting called by Benton, as were Russell Wiggins, the postmaster, and farmers Norris Rogers, J. P. Bailey, and E. C. Hunt. With others, they went door to door, church to church, through five counties. J. L. Shearon, who had been helping his father operate a cotton gin in town, was one of those who asked people to pay a $5 deposit to join the cooperative. He was hired as the project supervisor and would be the manager of Wake Electric Membership Corporation until he retired in 1971.

Early linemen Ira "Shorty" Lee and James Hall and manager J. L. Shearon posed outside the newly-opened Wake Electric Membership Corporation office, the one-story annex at the Wake Forest Town Hall. *Courtesy of Wake Electric Membership Corporation*

By August, the cooperative was organized and received an REA loan of $325,000 to build 132 miles of line to serve the original 137 members; there were plans for 250 more miles of line to serve 750 waiting members. Shearon moved into a one-room office upstairs in the town hall; a few months later the town added the one-story addition on the north and that was Wake Electric's headquarters until the brick building on Wait Avenue was completed in 1950.

One of the first hires was Ira D. "Shorty" Lee, and for many years until he resigned in 1959, he was the only lineman. "Me and Leonard (Shearon) did all the construction and maintenance. I read every one of those meters by myself every month for years and years," Lee said much later.

The Wake Forest Woman's Health Club met from 1946 to 1956, and the members often swam at the town pool. *Courtesy of the Wake Forest College Birthplace Museum*

The second meeting was a regular town board meeting where Dr. Neville Isbell, representing the Men's Civic Club, recommended the

town build a community center and swimming pool. The federal Works Progress Administration agreed to build them with the town paying $12,800 and the WPA $67,117. The town voters passed the bonds easily and the pool and community house opened in 1942.

They were for whites only—and there was a great deal of discussion about whether to allow children and youth from the mill village in the pool. There were vague promises of a pool and other recreational facilities for black children and youth, but nothing ever came of those.

Before the new pool, all the white kids in town and the college students swam and tanned and socialized at the Golf Pond near Sunset Rock on Paschal Golf Course, although it was then known as the college golf course. The college provided lifeguards and Philip Utley, the trainer, went by every day to pour a disinfectant into the water. Sunset Rock—where golfers tee off now for Number Nine—was a favorite place to take a date.

In his history of the college, Dr. G. W. Paschal, who gave his name to the golf course because he donated land for it when N.C. 98 was built in 1923 and took part of the greens, said the pond "was used once every season for a swimming tournament and beauty contest."

The Community House and pool were built as part of the WPA program in the 1940s, and the pool was renovated in 1978, just before this picture was taken. The Community House has changed very little since it was built and is still well used for meetings, parties, and voting. *Courtesy of The Wake Weekly*

Another item of discord was dancing. There had been an unholy holy war of sorts for years about dancing at Wake Forest College, with most of the state's Baptists saying they did not want their ministers trained at a school that allowed dancing. However, people would dance.

Louise Williams, known throughout town as Miss Lou, was part of the Crenshaw Hall family. She rented the small end room at the Community House to give dance lessons. John Wooten Jr. remembers she began charging 25 cents a lesson and he had to quit because his family could not afford it. Grady Patterson Jr. recalls that he and his sister learned to dance in the Wake Forest Baptist Church parsonage with the Reverend Olive's daughters.

The college fraternities rented the new Community Building for dances at $20 a night, and the college trustees and Baptists throughout the state fretted about them.

Kappa Alpha fraternity was established at Wake Forest College in 1882, but later that year the trustees banned social fraternities. They went underground. Other fraternities such as Delta Sigma and Phi Kappa Beta were formed and operated "secretly" off-campus for nearly 40 years. In 1922 the trustees voted to allow fraternities and in 1936 built Simmons Hall for them, hence the five separate entrances. The college tore down the historic North Brick House to make way for Simmons.

Dancing was not the only issue where there was a rub. The town still enforced the Sunday or "blue" laws, including one that banned showing movies on Sundays.

W. L. Glover, who operated the Forest Theatre, wanted to show "The Dictator,"

The Forest Theatre on White Street was a source of entertainment and news for students and townspeople until it burned in 1966. The billing changed several times a week, with a double feature on Saturdays and the Movietone News on Friday nights. In the 1940s, children under 6 were admitted free, children 6 to 12 paid 14 cents, and adult tickets may have been 44 cents. *Courtesy of the Wake Forest College Birthplace Museum*

Charlie Chaplin's satire about Adolf Hitler, on Sunday, April 20, 1941. No problem. The town commissioners rescinded the ban on Sunday movies the week before the showing, reinstating it a month later. Then for two other movies, not named in the minutes, they lifted and reinstated the ban until finally in 1942 they gave up and said theaters could show movies any day of the week.

There were no bans against college sports, which were followed avidly by almost everyone in town as well as the students. People came from all over the area to watch the Demon Deacons basketball team play Duke or Carolina or State in Gore Gym. And there were larger crowds who came to watch the football matchups in what was first called Gore, then Groves Athletic Field at the end of West Avenue. Baseball was as popular, and the highlight game of the year was the one between Wake Forest and State on Easter Monday, played on alternate years in the town or in Raleigh. So many legislators were absent from the General Assembly that day that they declared Easter Monday a state holiday to justify their absences.

Groves Field was converted to a practice field after Groves Stadium on the new Stadium Drive was dedicated by Governor J. M. Broughton, an alumnus and chairman of the college board of trustees, on Saturday, October 26, 1940. In that first game, Wake Forest played Duke and lost, 23–0.

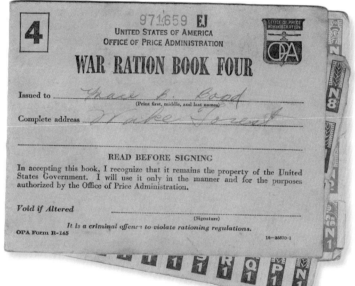

Ration book and stamps
Courtesy of the Wake Forest College Birthplace Museum

The new stadium (now Trentini Stadium at Wake Forest-Rolesville High School) seated 15,400 spectators, and there were two field houses, a press box, and a bar for serving food and drinks. Fifty acres next to the building was set aside for parking. The cost was $105,000, of which Henry Groves, a 1913 graduate who had succeeded in the textile field, contributed $25,000.

Of course December 7, 1941, changed everything. The college boys marched off to war, and the college fell on hard times with no students. Its salvation was the U.S. Army Finance School, with 1,200 officers and enlisted men, including 50 women, which began operating in August of 1942. By the fall of 1943, the school occupied over half the campus, spilling into the basement of the unfinished chapel.

Miss Jo Williams' cafeteria, which the college had built at the corner of South Avenue and South Main Street across from Wake Forest Baptist Church, was the mess hall for the officers and men and provided summer and after-school employment for a troop of Wake Forest teenagers.

It took the war to bring women to the campus. There had been a few women students through the years, daughters of faculty members, as well as those enrolled in the summer sessions, mostly teachers. Eva Belle Simmons graduated in 1888. Margaret Gordon graduated from the law school in 1927 and was the first North Carolina woman admitted to the bar. But in 1942, with male students scarce on the ground, women were admitted as full students.

The town board agreed to pay to truck in the sewing machines for the Red Cross chapter that met in the Community House, agreed the USO could use it free of charge for the duration of the war—Miss Lou was the USO director—and set special pool hours for enlisted men, officers, and their "wives and lady friends."

The commissioners were still meeting and deciding behind closed doors, and the only way town residents knew of the decisions was from the notices posted on a board at the municipal building where the truck for the white fire department was in a bay on the north side, the town clerk, police department, utilities superintendent, and the jail occupied the rest of the ground floor, and Recorder's Court with Judge Donald Gulley presiding met every two weeks upstairs. Wake Electric operated from the one-story addition on the north.

The town's electric operation was highly profitable. In 1949–1950, town property taxes brought in $10,000 but the electric department profit was $31,000. The town could afford to extend a few electric lines

Another impact of the war was the enrollment of women at Wake Forest College in 1942. The only male students remaining were under 18 or 4F. The 1944–1945 Demon Deacon Band, on the steps of Gore Gym, included Sophie Wall, the first majorette. *Courtesy of W. R. Wilkinson III*

outside town and buy back some lines individuals had paid to install, such as the line down to R. L. Harris' Forest Heights Service Station south of Forestville.

One of the most spectacular events of the early 1940s occurred on January 14, 1942, when the New York-Florida Limited train struck a Staudt's Bakery truck at the Royal Cotton Mills (Brick Street) crossing, killing the driver, ripping the truck into two parts, and tossing bread and debris everywhere. A bread box was hurled 100 feet to the top of a telephone pole.

Part of the truck was caught under the pilot wheels of the locomotive and caused it to overturn at the new underpass, coming to rest just inches from the brick building that housed Hardwicke's Pharmacy. The building had been rammed by another train accident in 1928, and in that the drugstore was badly damaged.

It was 1942 also when the town board discussed and then formed what was called the Colored Volunteer Fire Department, and that year it sent two firemen from

Cornelius Scheve attended the Finance School, and his scrapbook, which was donated to the Wake Forest College Birthplace, included this picture of the chow line at Miss Jo's Cafeteria. *Courtesy of the Wake Forest College Birthplace Museum*

Scheve's album includes this picture of a Finance School student leaving Oscar Smith's Electric Shoe Shop on North White Street. His sons ran the business for a short time after Mr. Smith died. *Courtesy of the Wake Forest College Birthplace Museum*

Gill's Pool room was also on North White Street. It was originally owned by Joe Gill, and Johnnie Hayes ran it after Mr. Gill died. A nearby restaurant was run by Louis Gill, and Edward Gill owned the barbershop that was also nearby where Benjamin Smith, known as Ed, cut hair until Schrader came to town and he went to work there. *Courtesy of the Wake Forest College Birthplace Museum*

each company to conventions. The town paid $80 for two white firemen to go to the Greensboro convention and $10 for two black firemen to attend the convention in Warrenton.

A year later the town would agree to pay $1.75 annually for each of the 15 members of the Colored Volunteer Fire Department, or Station #2 as it was called, for membership and insurance through the state association. Although the town board investigated the idea of buying a truck for Station #2, which was a garage under the North Taylor Street water tank, the truck the station got was an old panel truck, Matthew Williams remembered much later.

Frank R. Keith was named the chief for the white department, and Edward Alston was chief for the black department.

Station #2 was an important part of life in the East End, and it was an important part of the town's firefighting force. In both 1946 and 1947, and perhaps in other years, the firemen sponsored a fundraising carnival with the town providing electricity. At all times, the town commissioners ordered that the Station #2 truck be started each day—there were obviously fears the aging equipment might not respond when needed—and the firemen were ordered to drive the truck to the municipal building immediately when fire truck #1 had to leave town. A lot of the equipment anxieties were eased in 1948 when the town purchased a 1947 Chevrolet truck with a Barton pumper and the 1934 fire truck was sent to Station #2.

By the mid-1940s there were 19 fire alarm boxes (all in the white areas of town), alarms in each fireman's home, and a compressed-air fire whistle had been installed at the top of the water tank on Elm Avenue near the water treatment plant. It blew a different code depending on the fire's location. Everyone in town knew the codes and turned out to watch the fire or help.

Keith's Super Market was a Wake Forest landmark for many years. In this 1944 scene, the store on South White Street was well stocked with Christmas oranges. After a fire, Keith's moved to a new building on Brooks Street. The grocery store closed in 1993 and is now The Forks Cafeteria. *Artist: Sherry Allis*

The war may have been going on overseas, but here the town kept making improvements. In 1943, it hired the surveying firm of Arrington and Arrington, father and son, both named Thomas and descendants of Samuel Wait, to survey the town limits and number the 600 houses. Voters approved bond issues and new streets were opened—Woodland and Rayburn—and others—North College and South White— were extended and paved.

About this time a real novelty and something many families came to depend on, the Freezer Locker, was built on the new Roosevelt Avenue about where it joins Wait

World War II impacted Wake Forest in a number of ways. Ration Stamps and Victory Gardens were a way of life in those years. According to a *News & Observer* article in June of 1942, the work clothes modeled here by Elizabeth Seawell of the Agricultural Extension office staff were designed by Miss Willie N. Hunter for home demonstration club women and other rural women for wartime work in victory gardens and labor in the fields. The News & Observer, *courtesy of Barbara and Speed Massenburg*

Avenue. Farm and town families now had a way to preserve the hogs and cattle and chickens, the beans and corn and peas they had raised. Before the Freezer Locker, the alternatives were smoking, salting, or canning.

All during the war, there were no new consumer products: no new cars, refrigerators, stoves, or radios. People drove the car they had or walked, they wore the clothes they started the war with, and they saved everything for the war effort: the bacon fat from breakfast, the morning's newspaper, cardboard of any kind, and metal. The members of Boy Scout Troop Number Five collected and baled the paper and cardboard and scoured the countryside on their bicycles, searching for abandoned metal farm equipment. Everyone looked everywhere for metal objects and tossed them into an open railroad car that stood on a siding.

Day and night, trains carrying tanks, troops, and war material thundered through town, and a block away U.S. 1, still the major north-south highway on the East Coast, carried troop convoys, tanks, and Jeeps through town constantly.

With all the trains came wharf rats, which were a constant pest and health problem, as Army and town health officials often pointed out. Another problem was venereal disease, and the town government paid the $25 rent all through the 1940s for a clinic to treat it.

Meanwhile, the war brought better times for the mill village because there was a demand for cotton. The mill had been reorganized after the bankruptcy and was now Royal Cotton Mill with one L.

The minimum wage at the mill had been 18 cents an hour in the 1930s. In 1937 the first federal minimum wage act was passed, guaranteeing 25 cents an hour and

The houses in the Royall Mill Village were mill-owned until the 1940s, when the mill began selling them to the workers who lived there. The village remains a charming neighborhood today. *Artist: Maureen Seltzer*

a maximum work week of 44 hours. "I thought I'd gone to heaven," longtime mill worker Marlon Cole said. But there were also times when there was no work and men, Jack Horton among them, went to work with the WPA, building the Wake Forest Community House and repairing the rock wall around the campus that "Doctor" Tom Jeffries built. By late 1941, there was enough work at the mill to raise the minimum wage above the national requirement.

Now mill president Don P. Johnston persuaded the directors they no longer needed to act as parents to the mill hands and their families. The village was surveyed and subdivided into individual lots for each of the houses, and the mill began selling the houses to the workers. That first subdivision had 160 lots with houses on 88 of them.

The houses were offered at what seem very small prices today but looked enormous then. Claire Wall said, "I remember people saying, how in the world will we ever get it paid for?" Jack Horton bought his house for $400, and for the following seven years, $1.67 was deducted from his weekly paycheck.

After the houses were sold, the mill management saw no real reason to maintain the town, and in 1945 the General Assembly repealed the charter for the Town of Royall Mills. The Town of Wake Forest took over maintenance of the water system but made no effort to annex the area as former mill owners had feared.

It was also in 1945 that the mill was sold to two men who would both become U.S. senators, B. Everett Jordan and Willis Smith.

Down in Forestville, which had not been a town since 1915 when its charter was repealed for the second time, there was still a village with stores, a church, and a community life, although the pull was toward the larger town just to the north.

When the war ended, the future looked bright for the town, the college, and the area in northern Wake County. The college boys would be coming back to the campus, rationing was ending slowly, and Wake Electric could once more purchase the equipment and hire the men to install all the lines of wire for the homes and farms that had been waiting since 1942.

Since 1943, Wake Forest College President Thurman Kitchin and Robert P. Holding, one of T. E. Holding's six sons and president of the statewide First Citizens Bank and Trust Company, had been leading a drive to increase the college endowment and build more classrooms. They were planning for an enrollment of at least 2,000 students.

Wake Electric set the poles and installed the electric lines in the rural areas around Wake Forest in the early 1940s. *Courtesy of Wake Electric Membership Corporation*

Locally, Wake Forest people had contributed $126,622 to the effort. The architects' plans for 11 buildings had been approved; the steel had been ordered for the first buildings, and some had been delivered. The new college chapel was half-built.

The news came quietly, unheard by many at first. At 11 p.m. on March 25, 1946, a radio news report said the Z. Smith Reynolds Foundation had offered up to $330,000 each year forever if the college would build a new campus and move to Winston-Salem. The student newspaper compared the impact of the news to dropping the atomic bomb on Hiroshima. The only difference, it was said, was that the town still stood.

That spring was an anxious one for the college supporters and the townspeople. After the first shock, opinion among the state's Baptists began to slowly move toward the move and in July a special general session of the Baptist State Convention voted overwhelmingly in favor of the move.

With that decision, and with some friendly litigation which confirmed the contract for the move, people began to wonder how to raise the $6 million that was thought to be needed to build the new campus. The other question was what to do with the old campus.

It took longer to answer the second question. Even though the State Baptist Convention decided in 1947 that a Baptist seminary should be established on the Wake Forest campus, it was not until the spring of 1950 that the Southern Baptist Convention approved establishing the seminary and paying $1.6 million to purchase the campus.

Meanwhile, in town, the college's removal was a blow that seemed to threaten the town's very existence. It was not just that all the college jobs and families would be gone. It was not just that store owners like Ben Aycock did not see how he could sell enough men's clothing in Ben's of Wake Forest without the students. (He closed the store and was appointed the postmaster.) It was not just that the reason for the town had been the college, which seemed so permanent with its brick buildings enclosed by a stone wall.

People would also be losing something intangible yet real, something very precious. The sizzle of excitement on fall football Saturdays. The laughter of young men on the sidewalk in the early evenings. The clatter in the boarding houses at suppertime. The smoky haze and smell of hot dogs and chili in Shorty's on a winter

Now known as Shorty's, this popular downtown business was originally opened by Henry Edward Joyner as Joyner's. After a fire forced the business to move a few doors up the street, Worth and Buster Joyner joined the business and it was renamed Shorty's. The Collegiate Theatre was housed in this building for a while, but Shorty's moved back in 1962 and is still in business. This painting was done from a Joyner family photograph and shows the Chevrolet dealership on the left and Jones Hardware on the right.
Artist: Mary Benejam

The Fourth Annual Wake County Fat Stock Show and Sale will be held at the State Fairgrounds on May 5 and 6 under auspices of the Raleigh Chamber of Commerce. The show and judging of the animals will start at 7:00 p. m. on Wednesday, May 5; the sale will start at 2:00 p. m. on Thursday, May 6. All three beef breeds, Hereford, Angus and Shorthorns, will be exhibited on opening day, and offered to the highest bidders on May 6.

The Home and Farm Digest, forerunner to *The Wake Weekly,* was begun in 1947 and published every Thursday. It was edited by Peter D. Jones and the yearly subscription rate was $1.25. *Courtesy of the Wake Forest College Birthplace Museum and The Wake Weekly*

evening accented by the click of billiard balls.

It was also the pride everyone in Wake Forest felt in knowing that their town had a gem at its center, one of the premier colleges in the state and the nation.

However, although many did not realize it, the town had long been both a cultural center and a trading center for the area. Soon it would become an area dotted with industries.

In 1948, the Wake Finishing Plant, part of Burlington Industries, was built along the Neuse River on U.S. 1 south of town and soon employed 600 men and women.

In that same year the Wake Forest Chamber of Commerce was organized with J. D. Morris as the president of the board of directors and G. V. Barbee, Jesse Hollowell, Henry L. Miller, W. L. Glover, W. W. Holding, and Claude Matheny as board members. Mack Bridge, the high school agricultural teacher, was voted an honorary member.

One of the board's first actions was to appoint Miller to inquire about "more up to date service" from the town's first newspaper.

Peter D. Jones of Wake Forest began *The Home and Farm Digest* in 1947, printing it on his own small press. Ownership passed to G. V. Barbee soon after, and he renamed it *The Wake Weekly.* Nancy Cullom Harris edited it for a short while, and in 1950 Sybil Gulley (wife of Judge Don Gulley) and Inez Black, whose husband, Charles, was a college professor, purchased the newspaper.

The chamber directors, who met at Bob's College Inn (the Wake Forest Portrait Shoppe is in the location now) or the Durham Loan and Trust Company office, voted to buy signs pointing to the business district, discussed the possibility of a hard-surfaced road to Knightdale in hopes of drawing trade from that area, and pondered whether a cucumber market could be established in town. Farmers around Barham Siding Road near Rolesville were raising a lot of cucumbers.

The chamber also purchased Christmas decorations for downtown, hired someone to act as Santa Claus in the downtown area during shopping hours and put up prize money for the best floats in the Christmas parade, which was organized by the college or the fraternities.

The college, leave though it would, was enjoying a burst of prosperity and high enrollment because of the G.I. Bill. Veterans, many of them married, crowded into town with the younger male students and coeds. The 2,000 or so students often had to improvise housing.

Homeowners with a spare bedroom squeezed in two or three students. The college bought surplus barracks from Camp Butner and set them up next to the tennis courts on the former athletic field on North Main Street. Those were converted into apartments, but others next to the heating plant never had partitions. Trailers of every size were crowded into yards, near the barracks, and around Gore Gym.

Bynum Shaw in his fourth volume of *The History of Wake Forest College* said "J. A. West Jr. bought the last remaining unit of an abandoned tourist court in his home town of Wilmington for $50." That tiny house was placed in a collard patch growing on college property. Another student ordered a chicken house from Sears, Roebuck and spent a winter in it.

Jesse Hollowell opened his grocery store in downtown Wake Forest in 1933. His son-in-law John Lyon took over the business and changed the name to Lyon's when he built a new store in 1975. That business closed in 1991. *Courtesy of the Wake Forest Chamber of Commerce*

S. W. Brewer's Grocery and Meat Market on South White Street supplied meat to most of the boarding houses in town where the majority of college students lived and ate. The store also sold seed and feed to the farming community. *Courtesy of Virginia Brewer*

CONNECTIONS ...

Businesses

Small family-owned businesses served the community in the early part of the 20th century and some were run by several generations of the family. These interior shots give a flavor of the times.

R. W. Wilkinson Sr.'s general store operated in the Wilkinson Building for 50 years. Pictured are R. W. Wilkinson Sr., R. W. Wilkinson Jr., and Chester H. Wilkinson. *Artist: Gayle Blackerby*

Ira Otis Jones opened what became Jones Hardware on White Street in 1909. His son, Robert Leland Jones, joined the business, and after his death, his daughter, Margaret Jones Stinnett, stepped in. The business moved to a new store on Durham Road (N.C. 98) west of Wake Forest in 1991 and operated in that location until 2004. *Courtesy of Margaret Jones Stinnett*

Lynam Grocery & Market
MEATS AND FANCY GROCERIES
Phone 4426   Free Delivery Service
Wake Forest, N. C.   195___

M

No.
Reg. No.   Clerk | Account Forward |

37

Your account stated to date

William "Smiles" Lynam opened his store in the late 1930s at the end of North Main Street. He operated the store until he had a heart attack and died there on a Sunday morning in November of 1966. All of his six children worked in the store at some time. "Smiles" was well known for his special cuts of meat. He carried credit for those who needed it and saw to it that none of his customers were without Santa at Christmas. *Courtesy of Roy and Donna Lynam*

Ticket from Lynam's Store. *Courtesy of Roy and Donna Lynam*

5
1950–1959

The 1950s saw substantial changes in the social and economic life of Wake Forest.

The college was still enjoying the benefits of the G.I. Bill and continued to have high enrollments. The campus was cramped for space even before the new Southeastern Baptist Theological Seminary—President Sydnor L. Stealey, two professors, and 95 students that first year—moved into the School of Religion building in the fall of 1951.

From 1946 until 1951 when the steel for the first building in Winston-Salem began to go up, well-reported in *The Wake Weekly,* many local people continued to hope the move would not take place. The strong and persistent efforts of the new college president, Dr. Harold Tribble, to promote the move were unsettling to the community. Never before had there been an unpopular college president. There were even bumper stickers around town: "Tribble must go."

This culminated in an ugly incident in early March 1951, over an unrelated event.

Clyde "Peahead" Walker was a winning football coach, the most popular coach on the campus up to that time. Although the college Athletic Council had recommended a $1,500 salary increase for Walker, President Harold Tribble cut that to $500, although he later changed his mind and agreed to the full amount. At the same time that spring, Walker had accepted an offer from Yale to be an assistant football coach.

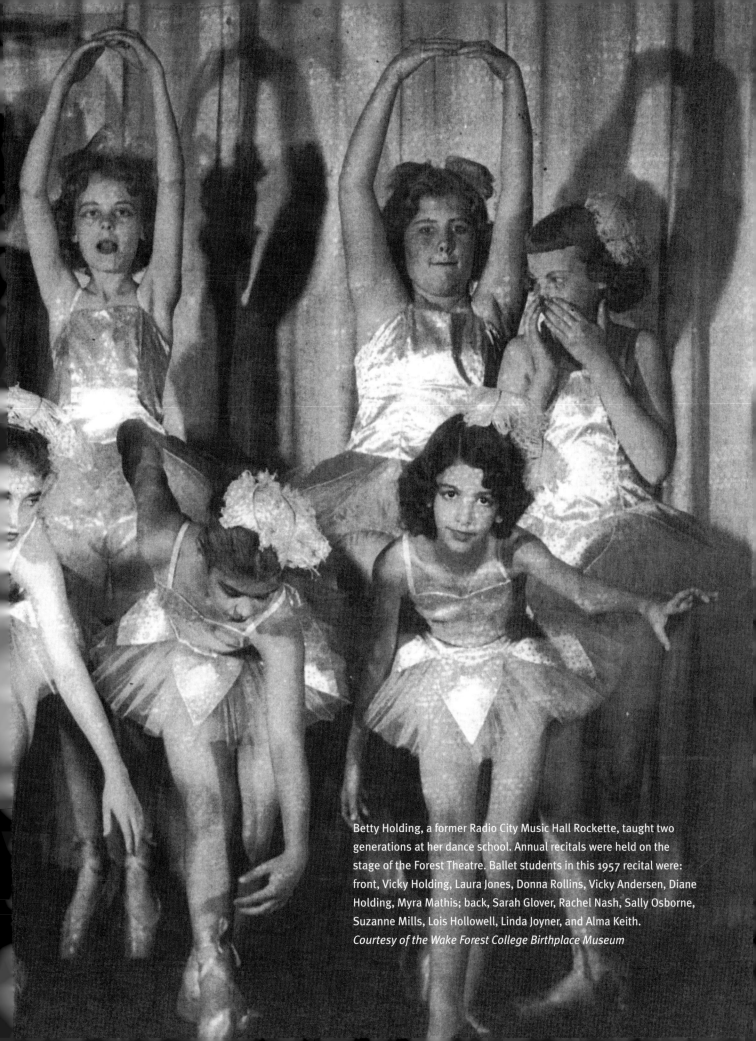

Betty Holding, a former Radio City Music Hall Rockette, taught two generations at her dance school. Annual recitals were held on the stage of the Forest Theatre. Ballet students in this 1957 recital were: front, Vicky Holding, Laura Jones, Donna Rollins, Vicky Andersen, Diane Holding, Myra Mathis; back, Sarah Glover, Rachel Nash, Sally Osborne, Suzanne Mills, Lois Hollowell, Linda Joyner, and Alma Keith.
Courtesy of the Wake Forest College Birthplace Museum

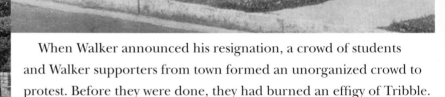

The Town of Wake Forest changed drastically when Wake Forest College moved to Winston-Salem in 1956. Southeastern Baptist Seminary had shared the campus since 1951, but the transition was complete when the name on the arch changed. *Postcard courtesy of Frank Drake; inset photograph by Rusty Forrest*

When Walker announced his resignation, a crowd of students and Walker supporters from town formed an unorganized crowd to protest. Before they were done, they had burned an effigy of Tribble.

Not only was the town waiting apprehensively for the college's departure, but another major economic fixture was also leaving. For 21 years, the first federal highway, the connector between Maine and Florida, had run through the center of town. Tourist homes, restaurants, and gasoline filling stations lined the route from the Franklin County line down through Forestville.

In May of 1954, the new U.S. 1 was opened after two years of construction, sweeping to the west of Wake Forest, Franklinton, and Youngsville.

When the college left in 1956, the town lost the $2 million or so the college and its students pumped into the local economy for everything from salaries to ice cream cones to hot dogs at Shorty's. When the highway moved, it took cash money out of the pockets of the tourist home owners, local restaurant owners, and gas station owners.

Every business leader in town was looking for a new source of money because they could see the seminary—certainly welcome for filling the campus—would not have the same economic impact with its older, more serious, often married students, some of whom left every weekend to preach at their home churches.

There were some businesses and industries. The Burlington Mills Wake Finishing plant south of town on U.S. 1 had opened in 1948 and employed 600 people. In

1950, what would be the town's major industrial electric customer opened, an alfalfa dehydration plant on Wake Union Church Road just north of Jenkins Road. It closed after three years because nematodes invaded the alfalfa fields, killing the crops.

There was the Evans lumber mill south of Forestville on the site of today's Wake Forest-Rolesville Middle School. Across the street, about where Capcom Avenue is now, there was a Waco feed plant, later a Purina dog food factory.

The mill village was changing. The mill ownership was now in Saxapahaw; the commissary was closed. Some of the residents found work outside the village and many people who lived elsewhere began working in the mill.

In March 1951, the Textile Workers Union of America, a part of the CIO, called for a general strike. The union wanted a 12 percent increase in wages for its members nationwide. About half the 270 employees at Royal Cotton Mill were union members. They worked three shifts, and the average wages were $1 to $1.06 per hour. The union wanted $1.21 an hour.

B. Everett Jordan was the president of Royal Cotton Mill and chairman of the North Carolina Democratic Party. U.S. Senator Willis Smith was an officer and stockholder in the mill.

Locally, contract negotiations broke down on March 16, and the next day about 60 union employees, who wanted Royal Cotton Mill to enter a binding contract with the union, rejected the ongoing national negotiations and set up a picket line.

That night someone cut the tires on the cars of the workers who crossed the line, and rocks and rotten eggs were thrown during the shift change.

On March 18, Wake Forest Police Chief Floyd Whitman Jr. reported about 300 workers from nearby mills where workers were not striking had come to town to join the picket line. He asked for calm.

For a time there was only shouting at the shift changes, but on the night of April 6 someone fired a shotgun into the home of a non-union worker. Also, someone threw a rock into another house, and the homeowner fired three shots at the rock thrower.

Events continue to escalate. On the night of April 25, three dynamite explosions shocked the mill community. There were five children asleep in Wesley Cooke's home when one of the explosions blew a hole in their bedroom wall.

On April 28 there was a full-scale riot. Armed men holed up inside the mill, and the N.C. Highway Patrol was called in to restore order. Legend has it that when the troopers arrived the violence was so bad they were scared to go to the mill and spent the first day hanging around "Smiles" Lynam's store on North Main Street, drinking Pepsi until things cooled off. It was national news.

Turner Ray and his grandfather, Priestley H. Mangum III, unveiled a historic marker on May 7, 1951, near Wake Forest. After the Civil War, the first Priestley Mangum perfected a terrace system that was widely used to manage runoff from farm fields. The marker still stands on N.C. 98 west of town. *Courtesy of Mrs. Turner Ray*

The heavily armed troopers restored order on April 29. The courts ordered resumption of contract negotiations. Warrants were drawn, accusations were made, and civil suits were filed.

After much political pressure, the North Carolina Supreme Court ruled against the union on November 6, 1951, and ended a period of turmoil that had been front-page news in Raleigh and across the nation.

In the mill village, the union and non-union workers—sons and brothers, cousins and neighbors—found ways to make peace among themselves and even today are reluctant to speak of the strike.

by Garland "Pete" Hendricks

In 1953, a large group gathered for their first year as Cub Scouts. Included in the picture are John Mark Long, Dwight Lowie, Billy Hunt, Billy Mangum, Ricky Harris, Ricky Frye, David Shearon, Tim Ray, Bill Parker, Bill Shearon, Walt Barnes, Harry Hagwood, Jimmy Jackson, Billy Mitchell, Barney Powell, John Rich, Harvey Newman, Russell Lipscomb, Buddy Murray, Bruce McDonald, Burt Lyon, and Garland "Pete" Hendricks. *Courtesy of the Wake Forest College Birthplace Museum*

Agriculture was thriving. There were several dairy farms, and farmers raised both cotton and tobacco. Wake Electric, begun to serve those farmers, was also growing. In 1956, the cooperative moved its offices from the one-story extension on the north side of the Wake Forest municipal building into a much larger brick building on Wait Avenue.

The new Wake Forest Chamber of Commerce promoted the downtown businesses in many ways, and the biggest celebration was the Fall Festival with a parade, a ceremony, speakers, and sales at every store in town. Those advertising in 1952 in *The Wake Weekly* were—from the front page through page eight; there was no other news—Edwards Pharmacy, Ben's of Wake Forest, W. W. Holding & Co., Harpers Shoe Repair, Arrington Electric Co., Mack's 5-10-25, Little River Ice Co., Hollowell's Food Store, Wooten's Hometel, Freezer Lockers, Smith-Hill Furniture Co., Cruser-Tynes Motor Co., Forest Furniture Co., Amoco Service Station, Service Chevrolet Co., Bob's

College Inn, Macon's Radio & Television, the Family Barber Shop, Glover's Radio & Appliances, Western Auto Associate Store, Keith's Super Market, B & E Cleaners, Luther's Food Center (featuring Elsie, The Talking Cow), Jones Hardware Co., B & S Dept. Store, S. W. Brewer & Son, Durham Bank & Trust Co., Edwin's Texaco Service, Geo. Bolus Dept. Store, and Miller Oil Co.

The merchants also advertised heavily to welcome the customer-members of Wake Electric each fall for the cooperative's annual meeting held in the auditorium of the school on West Sycamore Avenue. Until the high school moved in 1958 to the new building on Stadium Drive, the girls in the home economics department headed by Stella Forrest, the principal's wife, made the sandwiches or the barbecue served as lunch. The cooperative had 4,000 members in 1952.

Wake Electric, of course, strongly encouraged the use of electric appliances, all of them on sale in town. The Wake Forest Civic Club sponsored an educational program to inform people about the need for better house wiring and electrical safety to use the new appliances. Most homes were not properly wired, Don P. Johnston, the cotton mill manager, warned.

Although North Carolina and the entire South were segregated, there were stirrings. In Wake Forest about this time, several of the black teens who had to enter the Forest Theatre from an alley, order their drinks and popcorn from an alley window, and sit in the balcony, "accidentally" tipped over those drinks onto the white teens below. It may have happened more than once. Starr Glover could go to the movies for free because her father ran the theater. When she and her sister, Sarah, went with their longtime caregiver, Gladys Gill, they sat in the balcony. "I was always jealous of those who got to sit there all the time because, in my childish mind, they were the best seats in the house."

Many of the black residents did not even live in town because the town limits had not changed since 1880. It did not make much difference; services in the East End ranged from skimpy to invisible even inside the town limits.

Through the decades the town fathers had managed to ignore pleas for street lights, water lines, and fire hydrants until Bertha Perry met H. L. Miller. Perry thought black youngsters deserved recreation facilities as much as white youngsters, and she kept going to town board meetings with several other residents to say so. She was not making much headway until 1956, when Mayor Miller began to talk about building a swimming pool on the east side of town. He pushed and prodded in his polite, low-key way, always volunteering to be on the working committees, until a $30,000 bond issue was passed and the Taylor Street pool and pool house opened in 1959. (The pool is long since closed and filled with dirt. The pool house was incorporated into the Alston-Massenburg Community Center.)

Exuberant swimmers enjoyed Wake Forest Pool #2 on Taylor Street, which opened in 1959. *Courtesy of* The Wake Weekly

Wake Forest High School fielded its first football team, the Bulldogs, in 1956, coached by Tony Trentini. In 1980, a scholarship was established by the Trentini Foundation to honor the popular coach. *Courtesy of* The Forester, *the Wake Forest High School annual*

In the 1920s and for many years after, area school buses were driven by high school students. Drivers usually lived near the far end of the bus route and kept the buses at their homes. In 1950, the bus drivers at Wake Forest High School were Vermon Harrison, Wallace Shearon, Barbara Ann Ray, Lewis Nuckles, Junius Grady, Bobby Dockery, McDonald Allen, Buddie Looper, Tolbert Barham, Elie Keith, and George Mathis. *Courtesy of* The Forester, *the Wake Forest High School annual*

Students in Miss Pearl Ray's seventh-grade class dressed as favorite characters to celebrate Book Week: Phyllis Denton as Cinderella, Pat Dunham as Becky Thatcher, Jean Bond as Carmen, and Jimmy Cook as Johnny Appleseed. *Courtesy of Jean McCamy*

Even in the early 1950s dancing was a contentious subject at Baptist-owned Wake Forest College, but local teenagers kept things hopping in the Wake Forest Community House at the weekly Teenage Club and school-sponsored events such as this Christmas dance. *Courtesy of* The Forester, *the Wake Forest High School annual*

The 1957 Bulldog cheerleaders from Wake Forest High School gathered for a reunion in 2007 and posed with Cougar cheerleaders at Wake Forest-Rolesville High. Bulldog cheerleaders pictured here are Judine O'Brien Cole, Melba Hobgood Chalk-Edwards, Tonita Barnes Stephenson, Mildred Sandling Adams, and Lena Tabor Place. The 2007 Cougar cheerleaders are Elizabeth O'Brien, Kerri Smith, Ashley Redfern, Allie Garrity, Kristina Clark, Shelby Lee, Emily Lafella, and Meredith Shaw. *Courtesy of* The Wake Weekly

The Wake Forest Lions club hosted an event at the Wake Forest Community House in May 1950. *Courtesy of the North Carolina State Archives*

Forestville, or at least some of its residents, wanted to become part of the larger town. In some ways Forestville was part of the town. Electric lines had been extended down to R. L. Harris' Forest Heights Service Station several years earlier.

In the center of Forestville, Maynard's Grocery offered everything from generators to ignition parts, home-killed chickens, shirts, straw hats, plow points, fruit, vegetables, and the usual groceries. Later Charlie Lowery opened a grocery store in the same building, and people remember Charlie and Joe behind the meat counter while Hoye presided at the cash register. Napoleon "Chicken" Tingen worked in the service station tucked into a bay on the south. The Reynold Jones store and gas station, now a design shop, was across the road, which had little enough traffic that David Davis remembers riding his bike in the road. Howard and Geneva Pearson lived in the white house on the corner between Forestville Road and U.S. 1-A, and he ran a store that sold gas, cigarettes, candy, soft drinks, hoop cheese, crackers, sardines, and other light fare. Down the road, Forest Heights also sold gasoline and was a source of beer for college students and area residents. Some new brick homes were being built, and community life was still centered on Forestville Baptist Church and Friendship Chapel Baptist Church.

In about 1952, Ralph Cruser, who owned the Ford dealership on South White Street, strongly urged the Wake Forest commissioners to annex Forestville, saying it would be "a step toward attracting new business and industry."

In 1956, Ray Branson, a Forestville resident, asked the board to annex the area. Other area residents asked for a referendum and defeated the idea or fought it to a draw. This is the complete report from the July 26, 1957, issue of *The Wake Weekly*:

> One extra vote has the Forestville annexation issue up in the air.
>
> In Tuesday's election, 80 people went to the polls and voted but when the ballots were counted, it was found that 81 votes had been cast.
>
> Where the extra vote came from, no one is sure.
>
> The results were 41 against annexation and 40 favoring it. Eighty-five had registered for the special election; one died, three were out of town, and one sick, leaving 80 qualified voters.
>
> The Wake County Board of Elections failed to reach any decision at a meeting held Thursday afternoon.
>
> They adjourned to study the legal aspects of the case before ruling on it.
>
> They could call for a new election, which is what they are expected to do, or they may rule "no contest" and call it a draw.

Mayor H. L. Miller said late Thursday that the Board would probably make some ruling next week.

In 1958, J. L. Warren, who lived in Forestville and was a longtime manager at Central Carolina Bank, went to the town board with a petition asking for annexation. His request died because the town did not have the money to extend sewer lines to the area and it was not treating the wastewater it collected.

The sewer lines, built in the 1920s, went to Richland Creek on the west side of town and to Spring Branch and thence to Smith Creek on the east side. They were true outfalls: what was in the lines fell out into the creeks.

The untreated mess led to a lot of complaints. The ones noted in the town board minutes were from John G. Mills Sr. and John G. Mills Jr., as well as R. W. Wilkinson Sr. and W. W. Holding.

John G. Sr. was a professor at the law school and the attorney the town hired in the 1930s to buy the properties in town the county was foreclosing on because property taxes had not been paid. He lived on North Main Street, but his son moved out of town and built a house on the banks of Richland Creek.

R. W. Wilkinson was a prosperous merchant. In the early 1900s he moved the family home slightly farther east on Wait Avenue and built the four-story Wilkinson Building on its site in the northeast corner of Wait and South White Street. He moved his general store into the building—he would operate it for a total of 50 years—and his two physician sons, R. W. Jr. and C. T., had their offices there. Another son, Chester, operated a dry-cleaning store in the basement for a while but later, after some family dust-up, moved the business a couple doors north. R. W. Jr. and C. T. built matching brick homes on South Main Street and shared a driveway and a garage. They were always referred to by their initials, although Ursula, C. T.'s wife, referred to him as "The Doctor," capitalization definitely added.

W. W. Holding was a grocer turned cotton broker who built one of the town's biggest businesses, and his son, W. W. Holding Jr., put together the acreage south of town for the Holding dairy farm, ran the family cotton business and served on the Wake County Board of Commissioners for 25 years. He was instrumental in establishing Wake Tech, which opened in 1964, shortly after his death, as the W. W. Holding Industrial Education Center. W. W. Holding III, known around town as Little Bill, took his father's seat on the county board. He and his brother, Walter or Buddy, operated the family business until Bill's death in 1983. Farm operations had ceased earlier.

Owners of the Holding dairy farm south of town sold the herd of cows in the 1970s, but it remained a beef-cattle farm for some years after. The family divided the 900-plus acres after brothers Bill and Buddy Holding died. Some of it is now Heritage North; the western half will become a planned community of homes and businesses called Holding Village.
Artist: Wyn Easton

In the 1950s, the state was beginning to consider the condition of its streams and rivers and found that Wake Forest—like so many other North Carolina towns—was polluting its streams and river. You must treat your wastewater, the state commanded. It would take a few years.

One of the biggest lacks outside of town was fire protection. The town's fire trucks and volunteer firemen were for the town's use, and the commissioners tut-tutted every time a truck and firemen went to a fire outside town limits.

Tobacco was cured in log and timber barns, and they caught fire regularly. When they did, the farmer lost the barn and the tobacco because the only fire service was his family and neighbors with buckets.

Members of the Wake Forest Fire Department #2 competed in the 67th annual session of the North Carolina Volunteer Fireman's Association held at DuBois High School on July 12, 1957. *Courtesy of the North Carolina State Archives*

The local solution began in the spring of 1956 when several men, mostly volunteer town firemen, met to organize a rural fire department and establish the Wakette Fire Protection District. The Wake Forest Volunteer Fire Department was immediately incorporated with Willis H. Winston as chief and Raymond Keith as president. Albert Perry would become chief two years later. The first fire truck was a 1942 Chevy pumper purchased as Civil Defense surplus for $100.

In 1957, the town commissioners agreed to a request from the rural department and took over its administration. The county paid the proceeds from the rural fire tax to the town, which paid the bills and also donated surplus equipment to the new department. One was an old street flusher, which proved ideal for fighting brush fires. The same men, with one or two exceptions, staffed the town and the rural departments.

These were the years of the Korean War, the threat of nuclear attack, backyard bomb shelters, and "duck and cover" drills in schools. M. P. "Mack" Bridge, the agriculture teacher at the high school, was the local Civil Defense director, and at one point he was surveying all local buildings for those that could be used as a shelter for up to 50 people.

In 1958, the town board changed the way commissioners were elected. Since 1909, all town officials had been elected every two years. Going forward, elections would continue to be every two years but the terms for the mayor and commissioners would be staggered and would be for four years each. This is probably the time when the board opened the door and allowed residents to observe their meetings.

In mid-1952, the Wake County commissioners began planning for hospitals, one in Raleigh and others "in the outlying districts of the county," with one in Wake Forest. That fall there was a bond referendum which obviously failed. Voters had their choice: either additions to Rex (white) and Saint Agnes (black) hospitals or a new hospital to serve both white and Negro patients. Both bond proposals included four smaller hospitals in the towns.

In 1955 voters did approve a $5-million bond issue for a general hospital system, and in 1961 Memorial Hospital of Wake County opened on New Bern Avenue with 380 beds and 50 doctors on staff. The hospital buildings in Wake Forest, Fuquay, Apex, and Zebulon were completed by the fall of 1960, but putting them into operation was to prove difficult. That story will be in the next chapter.

Also in 1952, there was countywide interest in providing low-income housing, but at that time it would have been a town project with the town selling federally guaranteed bonds to build the housing. The town board never acted on that.

The town did enact a housing code and establish the first planning board, which then classified all the buildings in town as to their use.

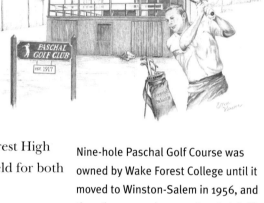

After the college left, the town profited from some of its facilities and land that the seminary now owned. The seminary sold 27 acres along Stadium Road in front of Groves Stadium to the Wake County school system in September of 1955, and about a year later sold the stadium to the school system for $1. The land became the site for Wake Forest High School, which opened in the fall of 1958; the stadium became the home field for both the Wake Forest High Bulldogs and the DuBois High Lions.

Nine-hole Paschal Golf Course was owned by Wake Forest College until it moved to Winston-Salem in 1956, and then the course became Paschal Golf Club. Its best-known player, Arnold Palmer, graduated from the college in 1954 and returned for a reunion in 2003. *Artist: Ellen Vanover*

1959 saw a momentous event. For the first time—and for the only time thus far—a Wake Forest native and resident became a candidate for governor of North Carolina. (Of course his son, I. Beverly Lake Jr., was the Republican candidate for governor in 1980, but he lived in Raleigh by then.)

Dr. I. Beverly Lake Sr. had graduated from Wake Forest College, where his father taught physics, and from Harvard Law School. He taught law at the college before he joined the state Attorney General's staff, and by 1959 he was in private practice.

He had appeared before the U.S. Supreme Court in 1954 on behalf of North Carolina to argue against school integration when the court was considering *Brown v. Board of Education*. Although he said at first he would not run because of lack of funds—the Lake family was distinguished but it was not rich—Lake changed his mind after Attorney General Malcolm Seawell announced his candidacy. The third candidate was Terry Sanford.

The Democratic primary—the deciding race in those days—would be in May 1960, and the anticipation and suspense were building as 1959 ended.

The Children's Parade was moved from hot and sunny South White Street to shady North Main Street in 1974. Here, costumed children assembled on the lawn of the Calvin Jones House. *Courtesy of the Kilian Family*

The fireworks show is one of the biggest attractions to the holiday festivities, and always draws a huge crowd. *Courtesy of* The Wake Weekly

In the 1970s there were a variety of games on the field along South Wingate Street, including this piggyback race. *Courtesy of Eugene and Betsy Adams*

CONNECTIONS ...

Fourth of July

The Fourth of July celebration has been a highlight of the year since 1973. Today, people from all over the area crowd into Trentini Stadium for the spectacular fireworks show. The next morning, more than 1,500 children, parents, and pets fill both sides of North Main Street for the Children's Parade and then move on to games and art in Holding Park.

On North Main Street in 2008, parade participants loop around three blocks extending from Juniper Avenue to North Avenue. *Courtesy of Stephanie Kaeberlein*

In 1995, Lady Liberty Bonnie Johnson and Uncle Sam Al Hinton presided at the fireworks show. *Courtesy of Al Hinton*

Who can spit watermelon seeds the farthest? *Courtesy of* The Wake Weekly

6

1960–1969

Wake Forest residents pitched in to help I. Beverly Lake Sr. in his failed effort to win the May Democratic primary, the first step on the road to the Governor's Mansion in Raleigh.

Lake made his position clear with a full-page ad in *The Wake Weekly,* stating: "The mixing of our two great races in the classroom and then in the home is not inevitable and is not to be tolerated." He blamed the NAACP for fomenting racial unrest.

Locally, many people viewed the election as critical and made sure everyone voted who was eligible. Mrs. Andrew Davis called for an ambulance and rode in that to the polls. Dr. C. T. Wilkinson drove his 92-year-old father, R. W. Sr., hoping his would be the deciding vote. However, Lake came in second to Terry Sanford across the state. Lake called for a run-off; Sanford won the state but Lake won his hometown.

The election and run-off overshadowed other events, including the bids—the winning bid was for $75,196—for the new water supply lake on Smith Creek. Work began in April, and the town was planning its first sewage treatment plants on Richland Creek and Spring Branch that would be completed in 1963.

Firemen needed warm water in the early morning hours of January 18, 1961, when fire tore through Keith's Super Market on South White Street. The difficulty of fighting a fire in the darkness was compounded by the sleet and freezing rain; ice coated the street, the hoses, and the firemen. Frank, Edwin, and Bruce Keith tried to rescue what they could from the office. The store was in two buildings owned by Tom Arrington and Wait Brewer, who would rebuild with

North White Street in the 1960s. *Courtesy of the Wake Forest College Birthplace Museum*

aluminum and glass fronts still visible today. Frank Keith, who had been in the grocery business since 1903 when he worked for Jesse Hollowell and S. W. Brewer at different times and then began a store of his own in 1913, said soon after the fire that he and his sons would build a new store on Brooks Street, a building that is now The Forks Cafeteria.

District Principal R. H. Forrest announced the county school system, which was separate from the Raleigh system, would build a gymnasium at the new Wake Forest High School on Stadium Drive. In 1960, the Wake Forest school district, made up of parts of New Light, Bartons Creek, and Wake Forest townships, had 7,330 students—5,500 white and 1,830 black. Only 2,606 students lived in the town limits.

A dedication service was held when Northern Wake Hospital opened in 1963. *Courtesy of Dr. A. N. Corpening*

The state agreed to pave South Allen Road to the new hospital, and that building soon became the center for much local exasperation. As other branch hospitals opened, those in Apex and Wake Forest remained closed.

The hospital was shut and inoperable in 1960, 1961, and 1962. At one point, a hospital staff was hired and then let go. Civic clubs and individuals appealed to W. W. Holding Jr., a county commissioner, and sent delegations to the full board of commissioners. There were petitions; there were meetings with hospital officials.

The problem was operating money; Wake Memorial Hospital was having a hard time competing with Rex, Mary Elizabeth, and Saint Agnes hospitals. The hospital board asked the county for more money in 1962, including $100,000 to open the buildings in Wake Forest and Apex.

Finally, late in 1962, it was announced the opening date would be January 7, 1963, and Sybil Swett was named the director of nursing. Five hundred and fifty-nine people went to the open house at the 20-bed hospital on December 30, with the staff doctors, Dr. George Mackie, Dr. George Corbin, Dr. A. N. Corpening, Dr. C. T. Wilkinson, and Dr. R. W. Wilkinson, in the receiving line.

In 1962, Dr. Mackie was named the General Practitioner of the Year by the North Carolina Medical Society, an honor everyone who knew him thought he richly deserved. He had come to Wake Forest College from Yadkinville in 1920 and never left except for the final years of his medical training in Philadelphia, where he met and married Kathleen. Together they were a formidable team.

In 1939, the North Carolina National Guard was called to service as the World War II war clouds threatened, and the local unit was billeted for a time in the Wake Forest school gymnasium. Dr. C.T. (Tolbert) was an officer in the Guard. "During the war, with

Dr. Tolbert Wilkinson serving in the U.S. Army, Dr. Mackie accepted the responsibility for the community as well as the student body and the surrounding countryside. He would have office hours in the morning, then spend a little time at the college infirmary treating patients, then either have afternoon office hours or visit patients in their homes," Grady Patterson remembers. "Then during the evening hours Kathleen would drive him all around the countryside treating patients. I believe he caught a few minutes' sleep between houses."

Many old-timers remember the long lines of patients lined up outside his office in their Faculty Avenue house or outside the office he had in later years in the former N. Y. Gulley house a few doors away.

He became the doctor at the college infirmary after the medical school left for Winston-Salem, and after the college left, he became the physician for seminary students.

The hospital was one of the community's focal points. *The Wake Weekly* reported the first patient—Henry H. Holding, 76, a grocer at Four-Way Cross Roads in the Purnell community—and the first birth—Ginger Gail, the daughter of Brenda Harrison Ray and Nelson Ray. Every week for years, the newspaper reported the patients' names and the births.

The newspaper also tied the community together with the local columns. Correspondents from surrounding towns and communities reported weekly about church and social activities. Mrs. D. P. "Gertie" Jenks, who sent in the Falls news, was a favorite with her pithy comments about neighbors and the Neuse River.

The "Local & Social" column was devoted to Wake Forest. It was where you learned who had visited whom, whose relatives were in town or had just left, and who had taken a vacation where. Newcomers, few as they were in the early years, knew they had been acknowledged a part of the community if Estelle Pearce called on a Tuesday to ask if they had had visitors or been on a trip.

Four doctors checked over the operating room of the new Wake Forest Branch of Wake Memorial Hospital. They are, from left, Dr. Albert Corpening, Dr. Nash Underwood, a dentist, Dr. George C. Mackie, and Dr. C. T. Wilkinson. The hospital was the last of the four branches of the county hospital to open. *Courtesy of* The News & Observer

The county had set up a housing authority in the late 1950s, and John Wooten Jr., the local board member, announced in 1960 that Wake Forest would have 52 units: 26 for white residents on the north side of Will Wall Road and 26 for black residents on the east side of North White Street. Construction began in 1961.

Wake County tried unsuccessfully to set up a library system in 1961, but all the precincts except Wake Forest rejected the necessary bonds that would have added 7 cents to the tax rate. As a result, the people of Wake Forest, who felt the lack of the college library and were served only by a bookmobile, decided to start their own.

Seventeen children heard Patty Ray read stories at the second weekly story hour for preschool children at the Wake Forest Library. The town's first library opened November 15, 1961, in the former Holding Cotton Company offices. *Courtesy of* The Wake Weekly

Catherine Paschal of Wake Forest, a director for Olivia Raney Library in Raleigh, arranged for the State Library Board to give the town a $3,000 federal grant. W. W. Holding Jr., who had just moved his cotton business farther south on White Street, donated the use of his former office for $600 a year. Mack Bridge and his agriculture students at the high school built the fir shelves. Nannie Holding suggested a book donation program, and the Wake Forest Woman's Club organized game nights at the Community House to pay for the rent and other expenses.

The library opened with 1,000 books on November 15. Library cards were 25 cents for students at Wake Forest Elementary, 50 cents for everyone in the Wake Forest school district, and $1 for everyone else. The Rolesville school district was soon added, with residents there paying 50 cents for a library card.

Although the shrunken community pulled together, supporting each other and worthwhile projects, there was a great deal of uncertainty and fear in the early 1960s. Some of that is evident in the history of the Wake Forest Garden Club, founded in 1924. Although there were 80 members in 1950, "In February 1962, the Wake Forest Garden Club was almost deactivated. The President (Mrs. Robert Llewellyn) said that it seemed the club had outgrown its usefulness to the community. It appeared that the Seminary lacked interest in the club, the members lacked interest in assuming responsibilities in the club, and the club was unable to attract young people to membership. It seemed that the club was at a standstill."

The Wake Forest Garden Club members traditionally celebrated spring by decorating hats with fresh flowers and parading through downtown. The hat tradition was revived in 2005, but without the parade. Garden ladies in the 1960s were: front row, Mrs. M. E. Joyner, Mrs. J. A. Harris, Mrs. George Mackie, Mrs. A. C. Reid, Miss Lou Williams, Mrs. Helen Johnston; second row—Mrs. R. M. Squires, Miss Mary Taylor, Mrs. A. C. Hall, Mrs. C. Y. Holden Sr., Mrs. John Brewer, Mrs. L. D. Gill, Mrs. A. V. Joyner, Mrs. L. F. Weathers; third row— Mrs. C. T. Wilkinson, Mrs. Kent Barbee, Mrs. C. S. Barnes, Mrs. R. W. Wilkinson III, Mrs. Carey Dodd, Mrs. C. C. Hildebrand, Mrs. John Apinis, Mrs. W. M. Satterwhite, Mrs. Bruce Cresson, Mrs. Ellis Nassif, and Mrs. Donald Gulley. *Courtesy of the Wake Forest Garden Club*

Flower-decked Mayor Vivian Jones, front left, installed the 2005– 2006 Garden Club officers: Jean McCamy, president, front right. In back from left are Mary Ducatte, vice president; Beth Kordon, secretary; Debbie Ludas, chaplain; Charline Tice, treasurer; and Maggie Goldston, historian. *Courtesy of* The Wake Weekly

Then in 1964, the industrial boom began.

At the end of January, John Wooten Jr. was able to call *The Wake Weekly* from New York City with the news that Schrader Brothers would build a plant to manufacture cylinders and valves in a 175,000-square-foot building on 30 acres of the former Jenkins farm on U.S. 1.

The town commissioners established the independent Industrial Development Corporation—Wooten, John Sanderford, Ellis Nassif, Robert Snow, and Paul Brixhoff—to sell bonds, buy the land, build the plant, and lease it to Schrader, who would in turn pay off the bonds while also paying all the taxes and maintenance. Wooten became the clerk of the work, inspecting the construction daily and paying all the bills.

The town did not annex the land. However, because the water and sewer improvements were underway, the town could run utilities to the plant with the county paying part of the cost.

W.W. Holding Jr. donated his empty downtown warehouse as training space. *The Wake Weekly* reported every company executive who moved to town, every step in the employee training, every brick in the plant construction. By the end of August, Schrader was in the new plant with 100 employees, planning to have 350 by the first of 1965.

Before the excitement about Schrader could die down, officials with Athey Products from Chicago announced they would build a plant on U.S. 1-A south of Forestville to manufacture large earth-moving equipment. It would employ about 250 men and women.

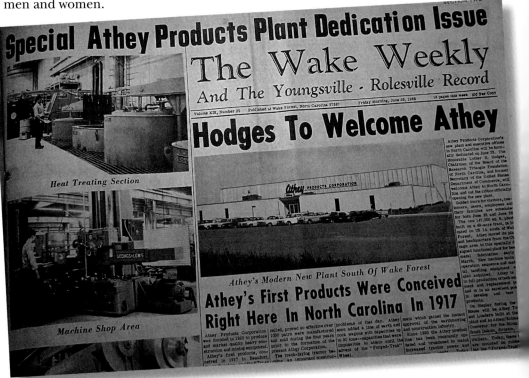

Athey Products Company, heavy machinery manufacturers, built a plant just south of Wake Forest in 1965. It was the town's second major industry; Schrader was the first. *Courtesy of* The Wake Weekly

Immediately south of Athey, the Neuse Plastic Company moved into the old Purina plant and began manufacturing plastic containers, including milk jugs. It employed about 45 people.

Right after Athey opened in 1965, ground was broken south of Wake Forest on U.S. 1 for Mallinckrodt, which would employ a number of Wake Forest area residents. Another plant outside town but bolstering the area economy was Diazit, which announced its plans in 1966.

The town had lost just more than 1,000 residents during the 1950s, but the new employment opportunities helped the town rebound from a low of 2,664 residents in the 1960 Census to 3,148 by 1970.

Wait Brewer Jr., following in the steps of his father, S. W. Brewer Sr., was elected mayor in 1963. With the help of Town Clerk Anna Holden, the first woman clerk, Brewer organized, filled out, and applied for all the federal, state, and local permits and grants to build the water treatment plant at the foot of the Smith Creek Reservoir dam and the new 300,000-gallon elevated water tank on South White Street.

Along with the water plant, a new reservoir for water and two new sewer plants to treat used water, there were several other changes. In 1964, town residents had new seven-digit telephone numbers and could dial Raleigh numbers without paying a toll. Wake County began a STOP POLIO campaign, aiming to inoculate all 180,000 residents. The seminary built a dozen duplex apartments on Rice Circle and Judson Drive for married students. The S. W. Brewer & Son grocery and feed store, in

business since 1917, closed. Shorty Joyner died. Brooks Street and South White Street south of Elm were paved. The Freezer Locker closed. The gym at the new Wake Forest High School on Stadium Drive was built.

In 2003 the old Athey plant was converted to a recreation complex called The Factory. The facility houses two ice rinks, an indoor soccer field, exercise facilities, shops, restaurants, and a meeting room.
Photograph by Sol Levine

Wake Forest was unlike most small North Carolina towns in the mid-2oth century in that it had no country club. Wake Forest College provided a golf course and tennis courts and there was a community pool; all that was lacking was a restaurant. Local residents made up for that by having dinner parties in their homes. These ladies were gathered for such an event at the home of Dr. and Mrs. Nash Underwood. From left in back are Lillian Faircloth, Caddie Farish, Jenny Brewer, Lelia Aycock, and Sue Byrne. Seated are Janis Underwood and Jean Fisher. *Artist: Kiki Farish*

Local artist Betty Bulla exhibited a painting of her children, Kathy, Grayson, John, and Neville, at the first Wake Forest Arts and Crafts Show. The Wake Forest Woman's Club sponsored the show at the Calvin Jones House for several years until the restoration made it impractical.
Photograph by Jean McCamy

Calvin Jones' farmhouse, which was the first building of Wake Forest College, was moved to the old ball field on North Main Street after the college left and preservation efforts were started. In 1963, local residents gathered for a "Rock Party" to pick up rocks on the grounds so that a lawn could be planted. Here, Ethel Crittenden, Eleanor Reid, Mary Taylor, and Virginia Hall take a break on the steps. *Courtesy of the Wake Forest College Birthplace Museum*

In 1968, the Wake Forest Chamber of Commerce, which met in various places but had no permanent office, announced plans to open an office in the Calvin Jones House. (It had been moved from Wingate Street shortly after the college left.) The exterior work to restore the house was complete, and there was $9,000 available for the interior. For several years the chamber sponsored the annual Wake Forest Arts and Crafts Show, which attracted artists and craftsmen from the entire region who hung their work on the bare lath walls. The chamber also sponsored an annual poetry contest, and *The Wake Weekly* published the winning entries in all categories.

There had always been one or two houses built each year in town, but the 1950s and 1960s saw the first subdivisions, all outside the town limits. Arlos Tarn began in the 1950s with Pineview Estates on U.S. 1-A almost immediately south of the town limits. Then Calvin Ray offered half-acre home sites in Lake Forest Estates north of town on the road to Youngsville. Shorty Lee, who had quit Wake Electric to go into business for himself, built houses

in his Cardinal Hills subdivision on N.C. 98 just west of town and connected them to town water. Nurney and Grace Bond were building three-bedroom, two-bath houses in Green Acres, and farther south, across from the new quarry that had been the Macon farm, K. S. Marshall was building Marshall Village. Town water lines were extended down U.S. 1-A.

More people meant more illnesses, accidents, and emergencies, and in response the Wake Forest Rescue Squad was chartered in January of 1965 with Gene Baker as the chief. Others in the squad were Red Wheeler, Charles Edwards, Phil Pearce, A. C. Hall, Boyce Medlin, Rodney Bright, Jerry Warren, Rick Newland, Dr. Robert Christoph, Maynard Hardwicke, Edward Perry, and M. P. Bridge.

In the years before the rescue squad, the two funeral homes that catered to white people—Bright-Daniel as it was called in 1965 and W. H. Willis—offered ambulance service with oxygen in their hearses. The Wake Forest Funeral Home operated by Carlton Hood Sr. with a black clientele may have also offered ambulance service.

A committee of W. W. Holding III, Mayor Wait Brewer, I. Beverly Lake Sr., John Wooten Jr., and Ellis Nassif had studied traffic hazards and recommended creating a bypass for N.C. 98 south of the town, building a railroad underpass on the south side of town, and leveling out the railroad crossing on East Elm Avenue.

The 1965 Lions Club Tigers, playing in the Wake Forest Recreation League, were: front, from left, Willie Harris, Jimmy Faison, Rock Harrison, Eddie Lee, Larry Warren, and Billy Wilkinson: back, Coach Charlie Padgett, Danny Crutchfield, Danny Black, Mike Wall, Steve Holman, and Assistant Coach Darrel Harrison. *Courtesy of Mr. and Mrs. William Wilkinson*

Jesse Wall, a local beekeeper, sold his honey and beeswax from this little store beside his Mill Street home from the 1950s to the 1970s. He supplied hives to the N.C. Museum of History and was a fixture at the N.C. State Fair. He was recognized posthumously by the N.C. Beekeepers' Association in 1981 for outstanding contribution to the beekeeping industry. *Artist: Karen Evans*

Dances at the Wake Forest Community House were a popular way to celebrate birthdays and, usually, several people joined forces to pay for rent, music, and refreshments, as in this case when four friends celebrated at this 1960s dance. *Artist: Kiki Farish*

A Wake Forest landmark and community center, the Forest Theatre, was gutted by fire on July 1, 1966, although men from seven departments battled the blaze. The three small shops tucked into the corner of the building were damaged. Margaret Stinnett remembers watching men hosing down the tar roofs of the buildings next door and across the street.

The theater not only showed movies but was also the stage for beauty contests and where Betty Holding, Bill's wife and a former Rockette, held the annual recitals for her dance school between showings of the featured film.

Another part of the town history had disappeared a year earlier when the Seaboard freight depot was torn down to make way for a parking lot that still exists on South White Street. The matching passenger depot on the other side of the tracks was torn down in 1964 and a small brick depot was built on the same site. The old wooden passenger depot had to be the one built in 1874 when Wake Forest College persuaded the Raleigh and Gaston Railroad to move the station from Forestville and paid $3,000.02 for the new building.

Fire gutted the Forest Theatre in 1966. The Fidelity Bank now occupies that location. *Courtesy of The Wake Weekly*

Prominent business and professional leaders in Wake Forest served on the Wake Forest Savings and Loan board of directors in the 1960s. They are, front row, from left, Samuel Wait Brewer Sr., Willie Satterwhite, Jesse Hollowell, Sam Sidenburg, and Bill Holding; in back, Judge Donald Gulley, William Royall, Dr. George Mackie, Dr. C. T. Wilkinson, Henry Miller, and Wait Brewer Jr. *Courtesy of Virginia Brewer*

Tournament winners at Paschal Golf Club were, in front, Richard Lee, Alice Soule, Janis Underwood, and Fate Wilkinson; second row, Dick Frye, Ludwell Barham, Buddy Holding, Twig Wiggins, Tommy Byrne, and Homer Wadford; back, Frankie Timberlake Jr., Tommy Byrne Jr., and Cameron Lee Jr. *Courtesy of Virginia Brewer*

Across town from the Community House, they were dancing at DuBois High, too, at this 1964–1965 Senior Dance. *Courtesy of The Lion,* the DuBois High School yearbook

Wake Forest gained its first park, Holding Park, at the corner of South Main and West Owen next to the Community House and pool that had been built in 1942. The land had been the site for the home of Dr. Solomon Pace Holding and his wife, Eva Dunn Holding. A number of people today remember renting rooms in the lowest level of the spacious house. On April 27, 1964, the land was dedicated to the town by W. J. Holding in memory of his parents and by Zua Mitchell Davis, whose former home still stands next door. The park was completed and dedicated on September 25, 1969.

The area also gained its first country club, the 18-hole Wake Forest Country Club Inc. begun by Tommy Byrne, Ray Faircloth, Ellis Nassif, and Jayne Keeter. The designer was Gene Hamm, who was rightfully proud of his work: "It almost reminds you of Augusta National."

The county school board was changing school districts in the mid-1960s. The last class at Rolesville High School graduated in 1965. Rolesville students now could go to Wake Forest High School, which had some extra capacity, but Rolesville parents and students, for the most part, preferred to go to the new Vaiden-Whitley High School. In Wake Forest, the sentiment was that people would prefer to consolidate with Youngsville, which was unfortunately across the county line.

Children clambered over the new play equipment in Holding Park soon after it was dedicated in 1969. *Courtesy of* The Wake Weekly

The wrangle about school assignment would last until 1970, when the old Rolesville district was split between Wake Forest and Vaiden-Whitley and Wake Forest High School's name was officially changed to Wake Forest-Rolesville.

Another complete change was coming to the county schools: integration. By 1967, 13 years after *Brown v. Board of Education,* the county school board had made it clear that would happen in 1970, and Wake Forest, along with other county towns, began to plan for what they hoped would be an untroubled transition. A Good Neighbor Council was formed in town, and there were committees set up at each of the schools—DuBois High School, which included grades one through 12, Wake Forest Elementary, and Wake Forest High School.

This was a very difficult time for many people. Only three years before, in 1964, I. Beverly Lake Sr. had run again for governor on a segregationist platform. This time he came in third behind Richardson Preyer and Dan Moore, but a sizable portion of people here and across the state agreed with him.

But in the fall of 1967, with the blessing of the county school board, the backing

of their families, and faith in God, five young women transferred from the comfort of DuBois to Wake Forest High.

Children busy at work in a first-grade classroom at DuBois High School in the 1960s. Mrs. E. S. Lucas was the teacher. *Courtesy of Bettie Murchison and* The Lion, *the DuBois High School yearbook*

"It was indeed a very rude awakening for each of us," Theresa Watkins says today. "It was a culture shock and more." Evonne Peppers, Jeanette Massenburg, and Pauline Battle "were forced to return to DuBois for fear of their lives and the safety of their families." Watkins and Rhonda Hood, daughter of the local funeral home director, would remain through two years and graduate.

Watkins said the majority of the high school teachers treated them with respect. "Of course, we could sense their true feelings but at least it was not shown openly. Pansy Sullivan, Ruamie Squires, Annie Bobo, and Stella Forrest were very compassionate and sensitive to our needs. I really believe these ladies truly saw us as any other students regardless of our color.

"Many of the students were cordial and some tried to make life easy for us. The negative students were those who came from poor families and felt threatened by us." She did add that "by the beginning of our senior year everyone had adjusted very well and the students were feeling comfortable in one another's presence."

The experience, she says, "has made me a very strong individual who is able to endure any storm in life. I've also become a strong spiritual woman who realizes that God is in control of every situation."

Lettering on the back of the building dates to its beginnings as a general store. *Photograph by Jean McCamy*

Fraternity members decked the house with anti-Clemson sentiments as part of Wake Forest College homecoming weekend festivities. *From a 1953* Howler *courtesy of Rusty Forrest*

Kathaleen Chandley's popular ice cream parlor, The Corner, served ice cream, soup, and sandwiches at lunch and dinner and was a favorite stop for walkers and bikers along North Main Street. *Artist: Linda Burrell*

CONNECTIONS ...

102 North Avenue

The building at the corner of North Avenue and North Main Street was built in 1897 by Dr. John Benjamin Powers as a drugstore. Through the years, it has been a general store, a boarding house, a fraternity house, a book store, an ice cream parlor, and is now home to a publishing company.

Debra and Marty Ludas bought the building in 2007 and renamed it The Forensic Press building, where Ludas operates his publishing business, supplying science textbooks and workbooks for schools. They are renovating the building as well as the historic Powers house behind it on North Avenue. *Artist: Ellen Vanover*

Seminarian Dick Stevens opened Stevens Book Shop in the mid-1950s and the building was filled, floor to ceiling, with books. *Artist: Dianne Ellis, courtesy of Dick Stevens*

7
1970–1979

The 1970s saw sweeping changes in area schools, highways, and housing, even in the size of the town.

When the three Wake Forest schools opened in the fall of 1970 with black and white students in each, the transition was so peaceful that newcomers to town never knew about the change.

But there was a loser. As in most communities, the black community lost the school they had supported, that had been a community center. No longer could they cheer the DuBois Lions to victory on the football field; no longer could they go to the gym/auditorium for the basketball games, the many programs, and the graduations that marked their children's progress. At least the school remained open and vital even though it was now the Wake Forest-Rolesville Junior High.

There certainly were undertones of racial tension, leading the Wake Forest Chamber of Commerce to agree with Ira D. "Shorty" Lee's motion not to allow any Christmas parade units with "political, racial, or controversial overtones."

On the other hand, the local Black Liberation Party had more basic concerns. Warren Massenburg, Ronny Williams, and Margie Gill asked the town commissioners to put up more street lights on North Taylor and Nelson streets, add more lighting at the new basketball court, provide faster trash pickup, and install another fire hydrant on Nelson Street.

This was also the year that the chamber directors set their goals to sponsor a calf show for 4-H youth, urge an underpass on the south side of town, explore the idea of a July Fourth celebration, encourage more homes, sponsor the Christmas parade and urge—

1976 was a year of bicentennial celebrations, including a parade in period costumes during the Miss Fourth of July pageant. From left: Lib Bartholomew, Missy Bartholomew, Robin Stenzel, Turner Ray, Ashby Ray, Harvey Newsom, Hope Newsom, Andi Lindsey, Paul Chandley, Pat Bartholomew, Kenille Prosser, Leon Stenzel, Jeff Stenzel, Geri Stenzel, Mary Pelosi, Carol Pelosi. *Courtesy of* The Wake Weekly

In 1971, Coach Larry Lindsey led his Wake Forest-Rolesville High School Cougars to the state 2-A basketball championship, the first of several consecutive titles. Members of the team were Joe Dormagen, Jesse Hood, Albert Jones, Brian Jones, Watson Jones, Mike Justice, William Lucas, Charles Merritt, Thurman Morris, Carl Moss, Bobby Parker, Martin Underwood, Charles Webb, Glenn Woodlief, and Frankie Woods. Managers were Chris Aldridge, Gary Toler, and Billy Wilkinson. Dennis Byrd was the assistant coach. *Courtesy of Glenn Woodlief*

again—the four-laning of U.S. 1, which was back on the state's active list of projects, now listed at eight miles for $4 million.

Downtown, the shell of the former Forest Theatre was torn down to make way for the Bank of Fuquay (now Fidelity Bank). The blackened shell had remained since the fire in 1966.

The year ended with the announcement that another industry, the Formex Division of Huyck, was to build a plant on 80 acres at the intersection of U.S. 1 and U.S. 1-A and employ at least 125 people to make fabric for paper mills. Down the road, at Wake Finishing, 1,300 people attended the children's Christmas party.

Wake Forest had its own version of March Madness early in 1971 when the Cougars won the state 2-A basketball title. It was the first state title for the school, though not the last. Coach Larry Lindsey, who had been lured from Youngsville High where he led that school's basketball team to the state 1-A title in 1968 and 1970, was to lead the Cougars to a total of six state titles.

The town's railroad era was fading. In December of 1971, Seaboard Coast Line announced that the midnight southbound passenger train, the Silver Meteor, would no longer run through Wake Forest, leaving only one north-south passenger train.

In May of 1971, Ailey M. Young led the voting and was elected the first black town commissioner. John Lyon was elected mayor, and Tommy Byrne and John B. Cole joined Dessie Harper (the first woman elected) and Dr. Carroll Trotter on the town board. They were a most unlikely group of revolutionaries.

By August they were agreeing that the growing town needed an administrator or manager, and in early November Mayor Lyon was able to announce that the first town administrator would be Julian B. Prosser Jr., age 25, who would begin work on December 1 and would be paid $11,000.

Cheering on the 1971 winning Cougars were Barbara Jones, Bessie Smith, Greyson Gates, Cathy Munn, Ellen Williams, Joanna Jones, Sharon Robertson, Sharon Massenburg, Shirley Wooten, and Debra Allen. Kathy Ward and Kathy Gates are not pictured. Basketball captain Glenn Woodlief and cheerleader Cathy Munn were married in 1974 and their son, Bryan, carried on the winning tradition as a member of the 1996 championship soccer team. *Courtesy of Glenn Woodlief*

The winter of 1971–1972 was exceptionally warm and some people delayed hog killing. Others who had not waited lost the meat to the warmth. Grady Miller with the Wake County Agricultural Extension Service said it would take a week or two of weather under 40 degrees for the salt to take hold in hams and other cured pork. He recommended taking the meat to a freezer locker.

By August of 1972 the town board had in hand a study for the annexation of six areas around town—Mill Village, East End, Cardinal Hills, Pineview Estates, Forestville down to Athey, and west along Durham Road to Schrader. All of the local industries and a large number of homes and businesses served by Wake Forest water and electricity were outside the town limits.

The Harricane, an area just west of Wake Forest, was notorious for its stills and production of corn whiskey, known as moonshine as well as a host of other names. But illegal whiskey production was not limited to that area; Wake Forest police officers found this still operating in town in 1974. *Courtesy of* The Wake Weekly

At the same time the commissioners were redoing the 1909 charter to reflect a council-administrator form of government and discussing whether to keep a provision that prohibited the sale of alcoholic beverages inside town and within a mile of the town limits. They left the provision out of the new version.

The annexation plans went nowhere at that time. In March 1973, Mayor John Lyon told about 250 people who had crowded into the former courtroom in town hall that there would be no annexation now, but it would be revived.

Governor Bob Scott came to town in the fall of 1972 to dedicate another new industry, AGA Gas on Forestville Road.

The first wavelets of apprehension about the impact of the dam on the Neuse River at Falls were being felt, and there were plans to zone the entire county, beginning with the watershed for that dam. Ira D. "Shorty" Lee of Wake Forest, a member of the county planning board, and planner Russell Capps received a frosty reaction at the Stony Hill Community Center.

The Neuse Valley Association, headed by Russell Dew and Rufus Forrest, had been organized by property owners to fight the dam project and the extensive recreation lands the U.S. Army Corps of Engineers was buying.

Many of the association members were like Henry O. Harrison, age 71, and his wife, who were hoping they could save their 200-year-old family home on Six Forks Road just off N.C. 98 about seven miles west of Wake Forest. It was due for demolition. "I feel like if some of the senators or somebody had known how long this place had been in the Harrison family maybe they'd have dropped back some to let us keep a piece of land to live on," Mrs. Harrison said.

At the first public hearing about the dam, not held until 1972, Forrest asked why almost all the recreation land was in Wake County with almost none in Durham and none in Granville. James Keith, who built the Yorkshire House restaurant near the lake after making sure the rules allowed it, only to have the rules changed, asked, "Why isn't the recreation land equally divided around the dam site? The land where it stops looks ideal—that land just happens to be owned by Gregory Poole—and then it resumes again on the other side of the property."

Rufus and Stella Forrest retired from the Wake County school system in 1978 after more than 30 years of service. Mrs. Forrest taught home economics at the high school from 1947 until her retirement. Mr. Forrest was the principal at Wake Forest High School for 20 years and then worked in the county office. After he retired, Mr. Forrest was very active in the Rotary Club and the Senior Center and served on the Wake Forest Town Board. *Courtesy of Stella Daniska*

Central Carolina Bank had been in Wake Forest since it opened a branch in the 1930s as Durham Bank and Trust. It had been a good neighbor bank, cementing that in 1965 when it named a local board of trustees headed by Southeastern Baptist Theological Seminary President Olin T. Binkley. Sometime in the late 1960s that group of good Christian men, which by that time included former mayor H. L. Miller and former chamber president John Wooten Jr., sweet-talked, blackmailed, and arm-twisted the bank officials into a deal they could not refuse: Build a new bank building rather than renovate the present one and make the present building available to the town as a library.

Nannie Holding and everyone else who used it agreed that the

The Wake Forest Public Library opened in the former Central Carolina Bank building on South White Street in 1973. *Artist: Donna Slade*

library, occupying just two rented rooms, was too small. The new Central Carolina Bank building at the corner of East Elm and Brooks Street opened in July of 1972, and in February of 1973 a committee revealed the plans to move the library to the former bank building, the Colonial-style brick building on South White Street.

Dr. Binkley and Robert Snow, the local bank manager, told a meeting of the Wake Forest Woman's Club that the bank would contribute $22,500 toward the project but the community had to donate an equal amount. The Town of Wake Forest had already agreed to pay for the operating expense and maintenance. Another $10,000 was needed for fixtures and had already been pledged. Once again the community mobilized for its library. Local businesses and industries donated hefty checks, and individuals sent in checks and cash.

It took only four months to raise the funds. In June, there was a check-passing ceremony with Mayor John Lyon, H. L. Miller, Dr. Binkley, Hazel Jones, Bill O'Shea, Bob Snow, and CCB President Paul Wright pictured, and the town had its new library.

Adequate safe housing was an issue—in 1973 one-quarter of the homes in town were substandard, often lacking full bathroom facilities or any at all—and that year the town board was happy to approve a plan for 50 public housing townhomes on North Allen Road with 30 single-family units for the elderly on South Brooks Street. By the time construction began two years later, the apartments for the elderly had been deleted from the project and the number of townhomes increased to 92. It would later be named Massey Apartments.

In 1973, the Wake County legislative delegation attempted to merge the two school systems, Raleigh and Wake County, after at least two attempts by the two school boards and a committee had failed. However, several county school board members led by Mary Gentry of Garner were opposed because the bill did not provide equal funding. Raleigh school children received $40 more in local funding than county children.

The controversy simmered. Pro-merger and anti-merger groups were formed. The local school advisory committees (they had a lot of power in the county system at the time) heard speakers and voted.

One very popular idea took hold in 1973. Janie Ali and Geri Stenzel approached the Wake Forest Community Council in February and asked for backing for a Fourth of July celebration with a children's parade, games, fireworks, and a barbecue supper with proceeds to go to the Library Fund. Until then, the week of July Fourth signaled a trip to the beach, and many industries and businesses closed for the week.

The two women went up and down South White, soliciting donations from the merchants. They found a number of eager volunteers, including Bill Shearon, Ricky Timberlake, and a large number of firemen who took over organizing the fireworks show.

An eagerly awaited annual event was the Home Demonstration Club's Christmas Tea at the Community House. At the 1971 tea, Marie Joyner showed her great-nephew, Paul Parker, decorations she made for the tree. She was ahead of her time in recycling a variety of cast-off items into ornaments. *Courtesy of Myra Parker*

The first children's parade was on South White, the games were on the elementary school ball field, and the fireworks were in the high school stadium, which was not yet named for Tony Trentini. It was a blast!

Greg Walton and the trombone section belts it out as the Wake Forest-Rolesville High School band parades. *Courtesy of* The Wake Weekly

The Wake Forest firemen who volunteered to clean up the stadium for the fireworks show were shocked by the trash in the stands and the general disrepair of the stadium. This was the beginning of an ongoing, decade-long effort by many Wake Forest High School alumni and other interested people in repairing and upgrading the stadium.

In January of 1973, Annie Belle Bullock and Geraldine Hall, members of the Alpine and Wake Forest Committee for Community Improvement, showed Mayor Lyon and Prosser, town commissioners, and county officials why the people just outside the eastside town limits needed help. There were about 60 people, 44 families, who lived on East Pine, Walnut and Sixth streets, North Pine Terrace, and Nelson and Juniper extensions. The average income was $50 a week. Nine families used privies because they could not afford septic tanks. Sewage backed up into homes and constantly seeped through the ground and stood on the surface. Lyon said the town could provide sewers only if all the property owners agreed to annexation or to pay all the tap-on costs.

These were hard times all over the country, and in Wake Forest the economic downturn was underlined when Royal Cotton Mill, now a part of Sellers Manufacturing Company in Saxapahaw, closed the mill doors in the third week of April in 1976. Many of the 229 employees were still without work the following year.

The town lost one of its most familiar and helpful employees. Guy G. Hill retired in 1976, 20 years after he came here from Stantonsburg to become the public works superintendent. He was in charge of all of the town enterprises, from the water treatment plant to the sewer lines to the streets and sidewalks and electric poles. And he was the de facto town manager for most of those years, taking good care of the town and its people. Hill went on to serve one term as a town commissioner. He died in 1994.

Several of the men who had been part of the Wake Forest Fire Department in the 1950s held a reunion in either 1978 or 1979. From left they are J. Albert Perry, Hubert K. "Doc" Denton, Raymond C. Keith, Willis H. Winston, George Timberlake Jr., Bruce Keith, Walter "Buddy" Holding, Woodrow Wilson, W. W. "Bill" Holding, Oscar Smith, McKinney Mitchell, and Edward "Ed" Alston. *Courtesy of the Wake Forest Fire Department*

One controversy was settled in 1976 when the two school boards agreed to merge the two systems, Raleigh City and Wake County, into one countywide system. The way to agreement was smoothed by the tact and diplomacy of Wake Forest's Sue Byrne, a member of the county and then the merged board of education.

1977 turned out to be a banner year despite widespread economic and infrastructure problems, including a natural gas shortage which shut down Athey for a time, and a bitterly cold winter that burst buried waterlines.

First, it was the year that construction began on the four-laning of U.S. 1 from the U.S. 1-A intersection south to the U.S. 401 intersection in Raleigh. At the same time a new section of N.C. 98 from the west side of Wake Forest nearly to Durham was being built. The new 98—only two lanes, not the hoped-for four—included a long bridge over the not-yet-complete Falls Lake and did away with the old bridge with its tortured turns on the west side, where several fatal accidents had occurred.

Secondly, the town received a federal grant to help ameliorate high local unemployment, $820,000 to demolish the old swimming pool and build a new 50-meter swimming pool behind the Community House, renovate the Community House, and build a new town hall. The town's contribution was to buy the land for the town hall.

The Wake Forest Municipal Building was constructed in 1909 and housed the town offices, fire department, and fire engine, Recorder's Court, police department, and jail until a new town hall was built in 1977–1978. This painting was done from a 1973 photograph. *Artist: Bonnie Brooks*

The Wake Forest Chamber of Commerce opened its first office in 1976 in the former train station on White Street. At the dedication ceremony, a railroad official (in checked coat) turned the building over to Chamber President Claude Matthews, Mayor Tommy Byrne, and Town Manager Julian Prosser. *Courtesy of the Wake Forest Chamber of Commerce*

Thirdly, the town was building a new sewer treatment plant on Smith Creek near the Neuse River, a plant mostly funded by state and federal grants. The town paid an eighth of the cost with a bond issue.

Fourthly, the town board voted to annex the west side out to Schrader. This first annexation was bitterly contested by Schrader and homeowners along Durham Road (N.C. 98). The town's position was upheld in Wake Superior Court and the North Carolina Court of Appeals, and it was only after the North Carolina Supreme Court refused to hear the matter in 1982 that the opponents agreed to annexation.

The East End, Glen Royal, Pineview, and Cardinal Hills were annexed without opposition in the latter part of 1977.

Fifthly, Southeastern Baptist Theological Seminary President Randall Lolley announced plans for new student housing and renovations to several campus buildings, and these plans helped convince the town commissioners to convert the electrical system from 4kv to 23kv. Town Administrator Julian Prosser called that vote "my biggest birthday present."

Sixthly, the town board adopted a complete zoning ordinance with subdivision regulations and set out a plan to reduce the number of mobile homes in town by enforcing standards for mobile home parks and requiring mobile homes be treated more like standard homes.

Hardee's, the first fast-food chain restaurant in town, was built on the site of the former R. W. Wilkinson Sr. house. Wilkinson moved the house around 1904 in order to build the three-story brick building, which still stands, for his general store.

By now, the town was moving aggressively to improve housing. It set up a housing task force, it was helping people obtain low-interest loans to improve their homes, and it was burning (with the owners' approval) houses that were dilapidated beyond repair.

Most of all, a federal economic development grant for the Pine Terrace area behind the Wake Forest-Rolesville Junior High would pay to rehabilitate the small homes, grade, pave, and gutter a real street in place of the dirt track and lay water and sewer lines.

This picture of Moses and Gracie Massenburg was taken by their son in 1956 after he was discharged from the U.S. Air Force. *Courtesy of the Massenburg Family*

One casualty of these changes was the Moses Massenburg store on East Juniper Avenue, also known as Gracie's, which had to be torn down for the extension of North Allen Road. Esther Shackleford, one of their daughters, had run the store since 1966 when her mother died. She remembered how her father slowly, painstakingly collected scrap lumber while he worked for the town until he had enough in 1939 to put up the building. He ran the store while still working for the town from 1939 to 1941, then turned it over to Gracie, who called it her "forget-me-not store."

In 1941, Moses Massenburg, who was raising a family of nine boys and two girls with Gracie, was paid $12 a week while the two white laborers, George Cash and E.L. O'Neal, were paid $19.

Shackleford put a mobile home on the lot after the old building was razed and ran the store from there until 1995.

Electrician Tom Arrington did not look convinced as Jimmy Holloway of Solid Sounds made a point at a meeting on downtown renovation. T. E. Holding III, a pharmacist and developer of Wake Forest Plaza, did not seem to care one way or the other. *Courtesy of* The Wake Weekly

The new Wake Forest Plaza built by T. E. "Tommy" Holding III and Charlie Bass on a new extension of Brooks Street was filling with tenants, first Macks, then Winn-Dixie. John Lyon completed his new grocery, Lyon's Store on North White, but he had to sell the lions—Tippy and Jane and their red cage—that he used in advertising because a 1949 state law, which applied only to Wake Forest, made it unlawful to display wild animals to promote a business. The big barn at Wakefield was sold, cleaned, and converted to an equestrian center. The state graded and paved the extensions of Elm Avenue and Franklin to reach Wait Avenue. The first meetings about a historic district along North Main Street were held. The fire alarm boxes at the street corners were taken out of service.

The town's slum, Barracktown, was about to be closed, and 20 families would lose their homes. Located out of the town limits east of North Allen Road, Barracktown was the end of the line for several of the army barracks that had housed GI Bill students and their families in the years after World War II. The owner, Seth Lester, had died and his heirs were anxious to sell.

1979 began with the announcement that a large industry was eyeing the Wake Forest area and wanted town water, sewer, and electric service. Within a week, everyone knew the name: Hewlett-Packard. North Hills Inc. and the Gregory Poole Company, the owners of the former Wakefield (John Sprunt Hill) farm between U.S 1 and Falls Road, N.C. 98 and the Neuse River, were urging the county to rezone 1,000 acres for industrial use, and Hewlett-Packard took an option on 230 of those acres for a plant to build gas chromatographs. Raleigh agreed to run a water line along Falls of the Neuse Road to serve the plant, and Wake Forest agreed to build a water tank at the corner of N.C. 98 and Falls to provide adequate pressure. It was estimated that the plant alone would double the town's population of 5,000. It would be "bigger than IBM," Mayor Jimmy Perry was to say later.

As for the current residents, the town could continue to help them because it had received a three-year federal Community Development grant of $1.8 million to improve housing and build new water and sewer lines and streets.

The decade ended with articles in *The Wake Weekly* that puzzled some and angered others. Four of the town commissioners—Terry Carter, Guy Hill, Fred Chandley, and Lyman Franklin—had met secretly without informing the fifth commissioner, R. H. Forrest, or the public. The articles said the four had agreed not to rehire Prosser, town attorney Ellis Nassif, and Town Clerk Carol Kinton, although no one was talking much publicly or for attribution.

Wake Forest-Rolesville High School's first soccer team was in 1975, and for several years the teams were co-ed. The 1975 team members were Greg Allen, captain, Dexter Horton, Jim Griesedieck, John Griesedieck, Sherrill Bartholomew, Allen Holden, David Meiburg, Doyle Andersen, Chris Bowen, Margaret Braswell, Philip Peyton, Randy Pelosi, Bond McCamy, Greg Williams, Mike Taborn, and Valerie Taborn. Mike Meier assisted Athletic Director Larry Lindsey with the coaching. *Courtesy of* The Forester, *the Wake Forest-Rolesville High School annual*

In 1992, the newly formed Wake Forest Cultural Arts Association's first Mardi Gras Ball was part of its membership drive. There were mask-making workshops for adults and children, and a King and Queen were crowned each year for several years. Here, an impromptu chorus line of mothers and daughters kicked up their heels. From left, Missy Bartholomew Lewis, Emily Holding Andrews, Lisa Bartholomew, Beth Holding Andrews, Cindi Holding, Betty Holding, Diane Bartholomew, and Lib Bartholomew. All the young women studied dance with Betty Holding, a former Rockette and local dance teacher. *Courtesy of* The Wake Weekly

Mardi Gras is not just for adults, as shown by St. Catherine of Siena Catholic School student Leandra Lee, who celebrated Mardi Gras 2007 with a carefully crafted miniature parade float. *Courtesy of* The Wake Weekly

CONNECTIONS ...

Mardi Gras

Mardi Gras celebrations have come and gone in Wake Forest. There were never any krewes but there have been parades, king cakes, and several different balls.

For years, St. Catherine of Siena Catholic Church held a Mardi Gras ball at the Youngsville National Guard Armory. It was well attended by Catholics and Episcopalians who observed Lent and a smattering of people of other denominations who just enjoyed a good party. Patty Roberts was in appropriate costume for the 1983 dance, which had a Dogpatch theme. *Courtesy of Biven Andersen*

The Mardi Gras tradition was revived once again in 2006 by the Downtown Revitalization Corporation. DRC Executive Director Tina Archer and her husband, Joe, were properly masked. *Courtesy of the Downtown Revitalization Corporation*

Freddie Green and his soprano sax added soulful notes to the 2006 Mardi Gras. *Courtesy of the Downtown Revitalization Corporation*

8
1980–1989

By January of 1980, the sentiment among the town commissioners had changed again. They voted three to two to rehire town administrator Julian Prosser—who had been left hanging in suspense—with commissioners Terry Carter and Lyman Franklin voting no.

But that was not the end of the story, because in April, during a Monday night special meeting, commissioners Fred Chandley, Guy Hill, Carter, and Franklin voted to fire Prosser. Commissioner R. H. Forrest and Mayor Jimmy Perry were Prosser's only supporters.

Tuesday afternoon, about 60 residents crowded into the meeting room at the new town hall for the continuation of the meeting, demanding to know why Prosser was fired. "I feel like we've had a death," Sue Byrne said. Chandley was the only commissioner to speak, saying he did not have confidence that Prosser would make rational decisions, "to act in accordance with the wishes of the town board."

Prosser's assistant, Jerry Walters, was soon named the new town administrator. Wake Forest voters indicated their sentiments in the next town board election by voting in Prosser's wife, Kenille, as a commissioner.

That controversy had just died down when another popped up: 50 additional low-income housing units the Wake County Housing Authority wanted to build in town. Wake Forest already had 154 of the 204 units in the county, or 70 percent. Aside from having the most low-income units in the county, town residents

Students burst from the door of Wake Forest Elementary School at the start of summer vacation. Wake Forest Elementary is one of the few local schools to remain on a traditional calendar after rapid growth mandated a year-round program to accommodate more students in the Wake County system. *Courtesy of* The Wake Weekly

Nearly 200 runners participated in the 1984 Rene Felton Run for Research in Wake Forest. *Courtesy of* The Wake Weekly

and officials were also unhappy because the most recent project, the 92 units at Massey Apartments on North Allen Road, were not what had been planned and the town approved, which was 50 townhomes. The other part of the promise, 30 apartments for seniors on Brooks Street, had been abandoned.

After town officials protested this latest project, William McLaurin, the housing authority chairman, told the planning and town boards it would not insist on building the 50 units—though the authority did later try to get some of the land rezoned.

This minor controversy became escalated when the head of the Greensboro office of the U.S. Department of Housing and Urban Development said the town had to accept the units to comply with the housing component of the three-year HUD grant it had. Despite aid from both U.S. senators, Jesse Helms and Robert Morgan, Congressman Ike Andrews, and Governor James Hunt, the town lost $1.4 million in community development funds.

That spring, Albert Height, a plumbing contractor, and his crew were hooking up 50 homes in the Mill Village to water and sewer, and contractors were about to pave streets in the East End, both areas just annexed to town. Gwen Smith, Barbara Hall, Barbara Upchurch, and Burma Burnette went to town hall to ask the commissioners if the streets were going to be left as they were, "all torn up," and Perry said the work would be finished.

Despite the loss, the work to renovate and rehabilitate houses, install water and sewer, and pave streets continued through the 1980s and the town continued to receive other grants. By 1987, Blanche Harding, the redevelopment director, could say that in 10 years the town had received $4 million from grants for decent housing and a suitable living environment and the town had spent close to $500,000 for water, sewer, electric, and recreation. The programs helped people like Eulah Harris, who lived in the East End and told a reporter she never had Sunday dinner, just cold cut sandwiches, because "I don't have no cook stove." Before 1985 was out, she had a renovated house with a complete kitchen and bathroom.

That was what did happen, but there were a lot of projects which, for various reasons, never materialized. Some of them were:

• The Hewlett-Packard plant on the old John Sprunt Hill (Wakefield) farm acreage. Lewis Platt, head of the division that would build the plant, spoke at the 1980 Wake Forest Chamber of Commerce banquet and said it would employ 400 to 500 people by 1983. Although H-P had purchased 230 acres, and although Governor James Hunt led a delegation to Palo Alto to help urge the project along, the project was delayed until it finally died from inaction.

• Holding Farms, which was planned for 900 acres on the farm owned by the Holding brothers, W.W. III (Bill) and Walter (Buddy), with about 414 acres zoned for residential single- and multi-family dwellings and the rest in office and residential. The development group included Cliff Benson Sr., founder of Carolina Builders and later chairman of the North Carolina Board of Transportation, Raleigh developer Bennett Keasler, and Jimmy Perry after his one term as mayor. They did buy and then sell the land where the post office, the library, the Northern Regional Center, the senior center, and Carolina House now stand on West Holding Avenue, but in 1989 they could not get loans to buy the rest of the 668 acres and the project went bust.

• Two large mobile home parks that were approved but never built. Neighbors stood up—even stood on their chairs—to boo the town commissioners after they approved a park that would have been called Smith's Point on the west side of Ligon Mill Road south of Burlington Mills Road. The 345-lot park would have included an eight-acre commercial area.

• The employment center that could have been on the Wakefield farm site and could have equaled the Research Triangle Park. Wake Forest, Wake County, and Raleigh officials met for six to eight months to try to work it out, but the effort failed.

In 1980, the N.C. 98 bypass was a project that the state highway department had been considering for at least a decade. Attorney John Rich told chamber members that year that it was the most important thing for the future growth of the town,

In 1999, Robert Boal, then 87, stretched before a competition. Boal became a world-class athlete after he retired from N.C. State, setting numerous world records in Masters Track and Field including a record in the 50.2-mile marathon. When Governor Jim Hunt established the Governor's Council on Physical Fitness, Boal was appointed the first chairman. He retired from competition at 90. *Courtesy of* The News & Observer

and the town's first planner, Jeff Baran, showed them a map of the proposed route. Town officials and business people were also anxious to have the four-laning of U.S. 1 completed to the north, but the date for that continued to slide into the future.

The Fourth of July had become a multi-event celebration and in 1980 included a three-mile Freedom Run, the children's parade, a fireworks show built around the quote from John Paul Jones, "I have not yet begun to fight," and a street dance on Saturday night.

From 1956 through 1963, Wake Forest College graduate and football player Anthony Trentini coached the first football team at Wake Forest High School, the Bulldogs. When they held their 20th class reunion in 1980, some of the team members talked about how much his fairness, honesty, and dedication had influenced their lives. Men such as John Rich, Sanford Bailey, and Jimmy Perry wanted to help their hometown, and they wanted to honor Trentini. About 20 of them met in October and decided to see if they could raise $10,000 to begin a Trentini scholarship fund. Within three days they already had $2,500 pledged. By December when the first banquet was held, the group had raised more than $13,000 and could award a four-year scholarship worth $4,000 to Tony Chambers.

A Wake District Court was gaveled to order by Judge Russell Sherrill in October of 1980, the first time there had been a local court since 1968 when the state reorganized the court system and closed the Recorder's Court, which had met on the second floor of the old town hall. The monthly District Court was held in the town hall meeting room.

The first Saturday in May 1981 saw the first Meet in the Street sponsored by the Wake Forest Chamber of Commerce. There were booths for 50 vendors, the Northern Wake Rescue Squad sold chicken barbecue dinners from a booth next to the former Del's Variety Shoppe, and the Wake Forest Lions Club members were in the store, selling hot dogs. The Pattie Johnson Dancers, the Dixieland Cloggers, and the Ronald Williams Mass Choir entertained. A week before, the new Historical Preservation Commission organized the first walking tour of the North Main Street historic district. For $1, one could tour 43 homes and look at the outside of the Calvin Jones House.

The town commissioners listened to experts that spring who warned of steeply rising demand for electricity and urged the town to join Power Agency #3. The town and 21 other cities and towns purchased capacity in four CP&L plants: Brunswick and Shearon nuclear plants and the coal-fired Mayo and Roxboro plants. By December, feeling the after-effects of the 1979 Three Mile Island accident, CP&L announced it would not build the final two units at Shearon Harris and would delay the first two. Instead of savings, the town saw increased electric costs and the average local bill for homeowners rose from $54 to $61 a month.

It was so cold that December that the traffic signals at the underpass malfunctioned.

Northern Wake Hospital was again awash in red ink, posting a 1980 deficit of $100,000, but Curtis Thompson, a Wake Forest resident and chairman of the county hospital system, said there were no plans to close it and its finances would improve as the area grew. Dr. A. N. Corpening and Dr. James Moseley were now the only staff doctors with local practices. The Chamber of Commerce was trying to recruit doctors who would use the hospital.

Southeastern Baptist Theological Seminary President Randall Lolley and his wife, Lou, shared black-eyed peas and collards with other Wake Forest residents at a New Year's Day lunch hosted by the seminary. *Courtesy of* The Wake Weekly

A number of professors and staff at Southeastern Baptist Theological Seminary served on town boards and were active in clubs and organizations in those years. Under President Randall Lolley, the school reached out more, hosting a very popular free New Year's Day lunch of black-eyed peas and collards in the seminary cafeteria and spending $75,917 to buy a new fire truck for the town.

In 1982, the Walter Kidde Company, makers of engineered systems for fire protection, bought land north of Burlington Mills Road, built a $6-million plant that would employ up to 250, and moved its headquarters here. The town extended electric lines, water, and sewer.

The town built its second park, this one on East Juniper Avenue and dedicated to Miss Ailey Young, who said, "Every community should provide access to certain things for its citizens. It should provide access to work, and every able-bodied person should work and should have access to a place to rest, to play, and to observe nature."

Falls Lake was nearly complete, and the rebuilt section of N.C. 98 between Wake Forest and Durham opened.

The first mixed drinks were sold in Wake Forest in 1982 at The Fountain of 1888, the restaurant Jimmy and Alice Ray opened in the former T. E. Holding Drug Store on South White Street.

In the first years of the 1980s, the town was in very poor financial shape. The property tax revenue did not stretch to cover all town expenses, so the commissioners

Henry L. Miller loved his adopted town and served it for 50 years, as a three-term mayor, head of the Chamber of Commerce, chairman of the Library Board, and in many other capacities. H. L. Miller Park was built in 1986 on land he donated to the town. *Courtesy of The Wake Weekly*

transferred money from the electric system to provide up to 28 percent of the general fund. It was so bad that the Local Government Commission told the town it could not hold a proposed bond referendum until it had balanced its budget and provided for reserve funds.

The success of the westside annexation in 1982 changed all that, and the town was able to pay all its bills, balance the budget, and begin to build reserves against emergencies.

After the town annexed westward all the way to Schrader, the directors of the Wake Forest Rural Fire Department looked into the future and saw it would lose more and more of the Wakette Fire District. The directors approached the Wake Forest Town Board with a proposal to provide fire protection to the town as well as the rural district. The negotiations were a bit bumpy at times, but in 1983 the contract was agreed on. Wake Forest became the first municipality in North Carolina to contract its fire protection to another agency, the newly incorporated Wake Forest Fire Department.

The contract led to a change on South White Street, where the two fire departments had matching fire houses with different histories. The rural fire department built its concrete block station next to Elm Avenue in the 1960s, while the town fire truck was still housed in town hall. In the 1970s, town hall became crowded, so the town first leased and then purchased Henry Miller's Circle Amoco service station and converted it to a fire station.

With the change to contracted service, the fire department directors decided a new station was needed and built the one on Elm Avenue that was completed in 1987. The old rural department station has had a number of uses, currently as offices, and the old town department's station was converted to serve as the Wake Forest Chamber of Commerce office.

It was early in 1984 when the Wake Forest commissioners voted unanimously to annex the Forestville area and the land along U.S. 1-A down to Weavexx. That company, Athey and Neuse Plastics, immediately hired attorneys, Dr. I. Beverly Lake Sr. and Jane Harris, to fight annexation. Roger Allen, president of Neuse Plastics, and some Forestville area residents organized opposition to a water and sewer bond issue that was needed to serve the area. The bond issue failed, although a later one was passed.

The town had recently numbered all buildings inside town limits and installed the green-bladed street signs without incident. Not so in the rural areas around Wake Forest when Wake County assigned names to what had been numbered state roads with rural mail route designations.

"Who decided that was Otis Knuckles Road? The name isn't even spelled right. My deed says this is the old Oxford-Raleigh Highway." "Where'd they get the name Mason Pond Road? This has always been New Light Road." "They can't get the names right. This has always been Stony Hill Road." Corrections were made, the outcry died down, buildings were numbered, and everyone from sheriff's deputies to mailmen to delivery people found it easier to locate an address.

There was a steady drumbeat of growth. The town approved planned-unit developments for Remington Woods on West Oak and for Tyler Run on South Main. Cimarron and Staffordshire subdivisions were approved as well as the townhouses at Weatherstone and the North Forest apartments. In 1980 there were 3,780 town residents; by 1990 that had grown to 5,581 with some of the population growth attributable to the annexations.

Former mayor Jimmy Perry was one of the developers for a shopping center then called Wake Forest Corners at the intersection of N.C. 98 and U.S. 1, where there was to be a movie theater, motel, bank, hardware store, savings and loan, McDonald's, Golden Corral, and service station. When built as the Market of Wake Forest, it had more stores but never did include a theater or motel.

Volunteers in bright orange vests became a familiar sight in the late 1980s as civic clubs joined the Adopt-A-Highway program. Lib Bartholomew, left, conservation chairman for the Wake Forest Woman's Club, led this group out for a Veteran's Day clean-up. Others helping were from left, Ruth Dancy, Joyce Board, Dixie Eckholm, and club president Hope Newsom. *Courtesy of* The Wake Weekly

Marshall-Stroud Dairy was sold in 1986 and later developed as Heritage Wake Forest. A Walgreen's Pharmacy now sits where the silos are in this picture. *Artist: Billy Farmer*

The cows were leaving. Holding Farm was no longer a dairy, just pastures for beef cattle, Caveness had not been a farm for several years, the Forbes farm fields were filling with pine trees, and in 1986 Emmitt Marshall and his son-in-law, Phil Stroud, sold their 1,100-acre dairy to Raleigh developer and builder Jud Ammons. "We really didn't buy it for anything in particular. I like to buy," Ammons said. He rounded up his sons on weekends and worked with them to plant pine trees all over the pastures. Ammons also tore down the silos and barns and emptied a particularly smelly pond next to Forestville Road.

Holding Farms Development Corporation presented at least two different plans for the old dairy farm but nothing went further than the planning stage.

The Jones brothers, Robert and Roy Ed, decided it was easier to grow houses than milk cows on their farm and went into the development business themselves. In 1986, Wake Forest's commissioners agreed to sell the subdivision on Jones Dairy Road 348,000 gallons of water every day, enough water for 400 houses on 240 acres. The Town of Wake Forest could not provide a sewer connection at that time, so the Joneses built a package plant and put a clause in all the deeds that the homeowners would not fight annexation in the future.

The town received a $60,000 grant from Wake County, half the cost, to build a community center, now called the Alston-Massenburg Center, at the Taylor Street Pool.

Gail B. Edwards decided to retire and close the town's oldest drugstore, the one that could trace its history back to the store opened by Dr. Benjamin Powers in the brick building next to the railroad tracks. T. E. Holding later joined Powers, then left in 1888 and moved south on White Street to open his own drugstore. Dr. Powers' son, Bruce, was the next owner. He sold the business to St. John Hardwicke, who moved it across the street after one train rammed the building and another nearly did. He sold the pharmacy to Edwards in 1946, and for the next 40 years Cola Matheny and other employees served up orangeades, lemonades, and chocolate sodas from the soda fountain.

In 1986, the Fourth of July celebration nearly died. The committee said it would have to be cancelled because there were not enough volunteers and because they could not use the stadium, which was being renovated, for the fireworks show. That announcement spurred Sue Osborne to say that she and others would organize the children's parade, Pinky Cooke to say she would organize art in the park, and the town recreation director Mark Williams to say the town would sponsor the games at the park and free swimming.

Volunteers stepped up too to meet another need. When a nutrition program at the Wake Forest Baptist Church had to be suspended in 1987 because of renovations to the Sunday School building, the seniors who had met there organized themselves into the Northern Wake Senior Citizens Association and began planning a senior center. The first officers were Rufus Forrest, president; E. G. Macon Jr., vice president; Tom Arrington, secretary; and Inez Hall, treasurer; with Miriam Fonville, Annie Belle Bullock, and Luna Marshall as directors.

A building committee was organized, and many other older residents became part of the efforts: Nannie Brandon, Worth Jackson, Thelma Wright, Mabel Shearin, Hope Newsom, David Hafer, Hattie Merritt, and Ida Holding among them. With the help of

Townspeople gathered to watch as an elephant strained to raise the tent at a traveling circus that set up in a field just outside town.
Courtesy of Patti Davis

the town, the county, and the state, the group was able to buy a site on East Holding Avenue.

There were several fundraising efforts, including a day-long festival with pony rides and other attractions. Even with the help, the group was still short of the total needed for the building in the spring of 1993, but they went ahead with the groundbreaking anyway. Their faith was rewarded very soon when Bertha Harris, a retired school teacher, gave them a check for $250,000.

Harris also gave $100,000 to beautify the town cemetery on North White Street and asked that her nephew, Hayes McNeil, along with Bob Snow, Jenny Brewer, Hazel Jones, Ruth Snyder, and Edwin Alford be named to a committee to oversee how it was spent. This was the start of the current Cemetery Advisory Board.

Following her wishes that the gift be an endowment, the town has kept the money in a separate account, spending only the interest.

Although there had been sporadic efforts and committees aimed at revitalizing the downtown area, the effort in 1986 resulted in the biggest changes. The brick buildings were cleaned with a chemical compound, new awnings were installed, and the town redid the sidewalks, planted trees, and installed new waste receptacles. A design team from N.C. State was suggesting ways to improve the downtown and insisting half of the White Street parking lot be turned into a park.

Another housing initiative began in 1987 when the Heart of Carolina Habitat for Humanity announced it wanted to build 22 houses on 10 acres on East Juniper Avenue across from Ailey Young Park. The project received a $70,360 grant from the state. Local and area churches and groups began volunteering to build the homes, and the town pledged to provide water and sewer and pave the streets.

The Habitat for Humanity house sponsored by St. John's Episcopal Church was dedicated in 1989. *Courtesy of Patti Davis*

The court fight for the southside annexation had gone on since 1982, with the town winning first in Wake County Superior Court, then in the N.C. Court of Appeals and finally, in February of 1988, the N.C. Supreme Court affirmed the decision by the appeals court and the annexation took place. Since then, all annexations have been voluntary and requested.

In 1987, the Wake County school system bought a site for a new middle school, 37 acres on the west side of U.S. 1-A, and Wake Forest-Rolesville Middle School opened in the fall of 1989. Teachers, staff, and students were pleased to leave the dilapidated buildings—in 17 years the school system had done precious little to repair, update, and renovate the DuBois buildings—but the move left alumni, the town, and the East End community wondering what would happen with the old campus.

Jimmy Ray was elected mayor in 1987 at a time that the town was facing increasing demand for baseball, softball, and soccer fields and recreation facilities.

Some of the land the U.S. Army Corps of Engineers bought for the Falls Lake recreation areas lies at the end of Old N.C.

Director Hugh McLean chats with two members of the Wake Forest Boys and Girls Club. First called the Boys Club when it met in the elementary school gym, the club changed its name to the Boys and Girls Club when it moved to Mackie Hall on the seminary campus. In 1998, the club was able to occupy its permanent home on South Wingate Street. *Courtesy of* The Wake Weekly

98, 400 acres on a peninsula. Back in 1979, the Corps had asked if Wake Forest would want to manage a park there, but there was no interest. Now Ray suggested it was time to look again, to see if it could be a location for the three more fields the Capital Area Soccer League said it needed in the area.

The Corps approved the concept for a park there, one that would cost $13.8 million to build, but the town could lease the land for one dollar a year. It was such an appealing idea that town voters approved a $700,000 bond issue in the spring of 1989 with $455,000 to begin the work on Peninsula Park and the remainder to build Tyler Run Park, complete Ailey Young Park, light two fields at the middle school, build restrooms at Holding and Forrest parks (half of Forrest Park is now the site for the Wake Forest Boys and Girls Club), and reclaim Rock Spring Park. Voters also approved $5.3 million for electric, sewer, and water improvements and downtown parking.

That spring also the Walter Kidde plant announced it was closing, moving to another location, and throwing 150 employees out of work.

Children scramble to fill their baskets during the Easter Egg Hunts sponsored by the town. *Courtesy of the Town of Wake Forest*

Competition is fierce during the Hoops for Wake Forest Three-on-Three Basketball Tournament held on a town street each spring. The proceeds benefit local nonprofit groups. *Courtesy of* The Wake Weekly

Volunteers, Tree Board members, Boy Scouts, and Cub Scouts help with the popular annual tree seedling giveaway, part of the town's program as a longstanding Tree City USA. *Courtesy of the Town of Wake Forest*

CONNECTIONS ...

Festivals & Events

As Wake Forest has grown, so have the activities. Fairs, festivals, and events fill the calendar throughout the year.

Barbara Massenburg, winner of the Peggy Allen Lifetime Achievement Award, waved to the crowd at a very warm 2007 Christmas Parade. The award, given in honor of *The Wake Weekly's* longtime editor, is one of the features of the annual Community Christmas Dinner where the Citizen of the Year and the Club of the Year are also honored. Artist: Kiki Farish

Santa waves every year at the close of the Christmas parade. *Photography by Rusty Forrest*

The arts and crafts show, Meet in the Street, draws up to 10,000 people to town each year. *Courtesy of* The Wake Weekly

9
1990–1999

In 1990, Wake Forest was still a small town—5,581 people—with small-town conflicts, but those conflicts between competing social, economic, religious, and cultural interests would sharpen through the decade as the town more than doubled in size by 2000, growing to 12,588 residents.

The first public conflict was over whether the commissioners or the town administrator would hire and fire employees. It began early in 1990 when Commissioners Edwin Alford, Hope Newsom, and John Mills voted not to give Town Administrator Jerry Walters a $750 merit raise while Commissioners Rod Byard and John Sanderford voted yes. There were several further clashes about personnel that year, some behind the scenes.

A building inspector resigned early in 1991, then asked to be reinstated, and Walters refused. The inspector filed a grievance which the commissioners heard in a closed session. The majority voted for the inspector's reinstatement, Mayor Jimmy Ray reported, but they very shortly learned they could not take action in a closed session and only had authority to hire or fire the administrator, the town clerk, and the town attorney.

Walters then fired the inspector.

The next clash was over a merit pay plan for town employees that Walters proposed to the board—which the employees liked—but all the commissioners except Byard called it "amateurish."

Late in January, Walters resigned at a called meeting, saying later he had been pressured to do so by some of the commissioners. Byard and Sanderford praised Walters'

A jubilant Wake Forest-Rolesville soccer team beat West Region champ T. C. Roberson three to one to bring home the 1996 state championship. *Courtesy of Chuck Hess*

professionalism and complained that problems were not brought into the open and "private networking" by some commissioners decided issues before they reached the full board. Assistant Administrator Mark Williams was named the interim administrator.

In March, Jake Wicker from the Institute of Government met with the commissioners, at their invitation, to discuss how to select a new town administrator. They also voted three to two to approve Mills' motion requiring the new administrator to consult with the board before hiring department heads or an assistant. Wicker predictably told them that vote was "inconsistent with the town charter" and just short of giving the board the power to hire and fire employees, a power the charter says rests with the administrator.

Undeterred, the board held two special meetings in one week, in one voting four to one to increase inspector Bruce Daniel's salary by more than $5,000 and name him chief inspector. Daniel had a job offer from his former employer, Granville County. Ron Doman, the parks and recreation director, publicly protested the unilateral pay increase, and Williams said he thought other town employees would view it as unfair.

One hundred and sixty people applied for the town administrator position, but the board had troubles with its selections. One man was offered the job but called back later the same day to say he had accepted another offer; another man selected had a poor driving record. Finally the commissioners agreed on Bob Slade, a former assistant county manager.

During those same months, the town board and planning board were dealing with a plan by Bbel Health Care to build a 60-bed nursing home at the intersection of East Holding Avenue and the future extension of Brooks Street. Former mayor Jimmy Perry, representing Holding Farms Development Corporation, which owned the land Bbel planned to buy, told the town board the company would pay half the

At a ceremony sponsored by the General James Moore Chapter of the DAR honoring Revolutionary War hero Colonel Ransom Sutherland, Turner Ray and Bill Gardner of the North Carolina Second Regiment Afoot fired a salute as Colonel Sutherland was memorialized in the rock-bordered cemetery behind the Villas at Wake Forest Country Club. *Courtesy of Lib Bartholomew*

cost of extending Brooks from East Holding and Bbel would pay half. But Perry asked that they not have to pay for the street until the rest of the street from the Wake Forest Plaza extension was built. Mills suggested waiving the construction of the street.

There were convoluted negotiations involving town attorney Ellis Nassif, and the whole question was tossed back to the planning board at one point to decide whether Holding Farms should have to pay two-thirds of the cost with Bbel paying one-third. Another principal in Holding Farms, Bennett Keasler Jr., said two-thirds would constitute a financial hardship, but the planning board voted to require Holding Farms to extend the street.

Apparently tiring of the lengthy dispute, Bbel bought a 5.5-acre site from Jud Ammons on Wait Avenue across from the water treatment plant, and began construction there.

There was a serious shortage of recreation facilities, particularly ball fields. The only town-owned ball field was at Ailey Young Park—all the others were owned by the school system or the seminary—and the lack of fields meant the men's softball program had to be cancelled in 1991.

It was no park, but the 23-acre former landfill off North White Street was level and available. The town donated the land to the Wake Forest Athletic Association in 1990

The first Wake Forest Artists' Studio Tour in 1996 opened with a reception at Chameleon Studio and Gallery. Some of the participating artists and craftsmen were, from left, Janet Rose, Kimberly Fentzlaff, Steve Filarsky, Peggy Taylor, Cindy Martin, and Donna Slade. *Courtesy of* The Wake Weekly

and agreed to spend up to $90,000 to build four ball fields. The group, however, at first did not have the $12–15,000 for a survey and later learned it would cost $250,000 to built two regulation fields.

The town negotiated with Ruppert Flaherty to purchase the 160-acre former farm next to the landfill, but the two parties could not agree on a price.

The town also lost its one lighted tennis court (at the corner of West Sycamore and South Wingate) because the site was needed for parking when the school system tore down the old Benton Building and built a major addition at Wake Forest Elementary School.

Marlon Cole, a lifelong resident of the Royall Mill Village, unveiled a marker designating the village as a nationally recognized historic district. Amy Pierce, a more recent resident, cheered him on. *Courtesy of the Wake Forest Historic Preservation Commission*

Ellis Nassif, 84, who had been the town attorney for 27 years, announced in 1991 that he would retire from that job and reduce his workload at his Raleigh law practice. He came to Wake Forest College in 1926 and graduated from the law school in 1929. He and his wife, Elizabeth, lived in the stone house built by his father-in-law, George Bolus, on Elm Avenue next to the water treatment plant.

In the 1970s, Nassif walked down to the town board meetings in the old courtroom on the second floor of the municipal building in his slippers with a sweater in place of his suit jacket. He sometimes dozed while sitting in one of the creaky wooden seats, but he was always alert when needed. During the 1980s, when there was less agreement and more controversy on and about the town board, he always appeared in a suit and shined shoes and never dozed.

In 1990, Carolina Telephone bought 70 acres on U.S. 1 just across the line in Franklin County and announced it would move its headquarters and 400 employees here from Tarboro. U.S. 1 from Raleigh north to the Franklin County line was renamed Capital Boulevard. Jones Hardware moved from downtown, where it had been for 84 years, to Durham Road. After Mill Village residents protested, Glen Royal Mills Partners backed down from a plan to convert the old Royal Cotton Mills building and site into an industrial park; and, in a separate venture, Jim Adams and Steve Gould rehabilitated the old company store at the mill, turning it into three apartments, and the town assisted by applying for a $66,000 federal grant.

A totally volunteer organization, the Northern Wake Rescue and EMS, which operated from a building on East Holding Avenue and from the former fire station in Rolesville, was experiencing a host of problems in the early 1990s—dissension among the volunteers, a decline in contributions, and some dissatisfaction with the service. Although the members of Northern Wake Rescue continued to provide a much-needed service, the problems persisted even with intervention and mediation by officials from Wake Forest and Rolesville as well as many concerned residents.

While the rest of Wake Forest was beginning to prosper, there was a black hole in the middle of the East End, the 17-acre campus that had been the DuBois High School, then the Wake Forest-Rolesville Junior High and later the WF-R Middle School. After the new middle school on South Main Street opened in the fall of 1989, the buildings were boarded up and left to the ravages of weather, neglect, and graffiti.

There was also ever-present concern about another local institution, Northern Wake Hospital on South Allen Road, because in some past years its balance sheet was blood red. It did report a profit of $300,000 for 1989–1990 and had five local doctors on staff.

Since the early 1980s, after it was apparent that Hewlett-Packard would never build on the Wakefield farm property, Wake Forest and Raleigh had been eyeing the

After Wake Forest hosted 26 members of the Russian Balalaika Orchestra and folk dancers for four days, Mayor Jimmy Ray accepted a gift to the town from the Russians.
Courtesy of The Wake Weekly

3,000 acres owned by North Hills, Inc. and Duke University for future expansion. Raleigh could serve it with water; Wake Forest could serve the eastern two-thirds with sewer. Wake Forest Planner Chip Russell recommended the town extend sewer lines to claim it for the town, saying it would be the town's best investment.

Mayor Jimmy Ray was continuing to pursue federal funding for Peninsula Park, the 400 acres at the end of Old N.C. 98, and in July of 1991 Congress voted $300,000 for the project. But at the end of the year, shortly after Ray was elected to a second term, the U.S. Army Corps of Engineers announced it would

The early communicants of St. Catherine of Siena Catholic Church first met in the home of Mr. and Mrs. George Bolus, then in a converted rail car known as the Saint Peter Catholic Chapel Car. A stone church was built on South Main Street in 1939 and served the congregation until 1997 when a large new church was built on West Holding Avenue.
Courtesy of St. Catherine of Siena Catholic Church

not participate in developing the park. That decision meant the town would have to pay for half the estimated cost of $15 million if it wanted the park. Ray reluctantly abandoned his dream. After a lot of dithering, the town board agreed in 1992 to divert some of the 1989 bonds for the park to build three ball fields at the former landfill, now designated as the northside park.

In 1992, 15 years after the section of Capital Boulevard between Wake Forest and Raleigh had been four-laned, the state Department of Transportation finally awarded the bid to four-lane U.S. 1 north from South Main Street to an existing four-lane section between Youngsville and Franklinton. The $8.2-million contract included realigning Stadium Drive and Harris Road to meet, respectively, Jenkins Road and Purnell Road.

DOT's 1992 plan for the N.C. 98 bypass was set to begin about 2000 and cost $19 million. Ground was broken for the Northern Loop Expressway, now I-540.

There was an overwhelming vote locally, 81 percent, for toll-free telephone calls to every part of Wake County. The high school and middle school had high long-distance bills because the administrators and teachers had to call to the Knightdale, Wendell, and Zebulon telephone areas to reach parents and students.

January of 1993 saw the town rezoning 165 acres for Steve Gould's Olde Mill Stream subdivision, the largest up to that time. Soon afterward, the Jones brothers said their subdivision, Jones Dairy, would add another 600 homes on 300 acres, again using Wake Forest water.

Although healthy in 1990, by 1993 Northern Wake Hospital was in serious trouble, with only an average of five patients per day in the 20-bed facility. Converting it to a long-term care facility was investigated and found not to be a viable alternative, and it was closed in 1994 although it was operated as a day hospital for two years.

The Wake Forest Fire Department hired its first paid staff in 1993, two firefighters and a supervisor.

Town Manager Bob Slade—he had had the title changed in 1992 to reflect the correct name for the position—resigned under some pressure in January 1993. Mark Williams was again named the interim town manager until he was hired as the town manager in May. Greg Harrington was sworn in as police chief in 1993, and Susan Simpson had been hired to head the parks and recreation department in 1992.

A new mayor, Dick Monteith, was elected in November 1993 along with two new commissioners, Joseph Cooke and Richard Finke. Bob Hill, Mac Turner, and John Sanderford were the other commissioners.

It was a contentious group. Williams said publicly that a lack of communication between the commissioners and the commissioners and staff was "a boil that keeps festering." Monteith and Hill were often at odds; at least one meeting had to be cut short because Monteith and Finke were arguing about telephone messages; Finke and Turner consistently voted against residential developments, saying the town should conserve its water for economic development; and by mid-1995 Turner and town attorney Eric Vernon were engaging in shouting matches. One was sparked at the end of the May 25 meeting when Turner walked by Vernon and said, "Dumb damn lawyer."

The commissioners were often at odds with their own advisory planning board. Three times from 1994 through 1996, Inez Mercer filed a request to operate a bed and breakfast in her North Main Street home. The planning board approved it each time; the town board listened to some neighbors and rejected it three times.

DOT hosted a workshop in late 1994 about the N.C. 98 bypass with maps showing two possible routes and set a construction date in 1997.

Seminary President Paige Patterson and the trustees were attempting to realize some profit from the large amount of land they had purchased from the college along with the campus and asked the town to rezone land along Capital Boulevard for a shopping center. The town board said no early in 1995.

Although they agreed Wake Forest needed a new library—the old bank building on South White Street was woefully inadequate by now—the town and the county could not agree on a site. Town officials wanted it on South White near the water

John Dean reached a milestone in March of 1998 by becoming the first WF-R athlete to earn a state championship at the 4A level. Dean aced the 100-yard butterfly after swimming his lifetime best time. In the 1990s, Wake Forest-Rolesville also had two individual state titles in wrestling, won by Jay Reagan and Kevin Stanley. *Courtesy of* The Wake Weekly

The new Wake Forest Library on Holding Avenue was dedicated in April of 1997. Among those celebrating were, from left, Ruamie Squires, Hugh Nourse, Betty Ann Wilkinson, Hazel Jones, Connie Nourse, and Shirley Wooten. *Courtesy of the Wake Forest Chamber of Commerce*

tower on land it owned, and the county's choice was a site next to the post office.

Wake Forest people were shocked in July when Raleigh agreed to the request from North Hills, Inc. and Duke University to annex Wakefield. Wake Forest's mayor and staff members had proposed providing sewer service on the east (Capital Boulevard) side of the tract first and extending service as the town began receiving revenue. North Hills, however, preferred to first develop the west side next to Falls of Neuse Road. They chose Raleigh after the city agreed to serve that area, bearing the cost of building a sewer line from U.S. 401 at the Neuse River, over to and under Capital Boulevard and then up Richland Creek.

The town board did approve the 396-apartment complex on Capital Boulevard, which was named Caveness Apartments and was the town's largest commercial contributor to the tax base for several years. They also hired architect Matt Hale to draw plans to renovate the old town hall, empty for seven years, for the planning and inspections department.

Increasing tensions were felt between the town and the seminary under President Patterson. *The Wake Weekly* reprinted an editorial from the *Biblical Recorder* which said Patterson was using "the secular political process to capture other things, starting with the town of Wake Forest" and criticized the seminary's involvement in town elections. Letters about the editorial filled the local newspaper pages for several weeks.

The 1995 election for three seats on the town board brought out 11 candidates and nearly 400 new voters registered to be able to have a say. Commissioner Bob Hill was reelected, and former town engineer Al Hinton and seminary professor Dan Heimbach were elected to their first terms. Commissioner Joseph Cooke resigned early in 1996 and the town board chose schoolteacher Velma Boyd to serve out his term.

DOT was still changing the bypass plans, which had now been reduced to two lanes, later revised again to four. Monteith was able to persuade DOT to build the section from Jones Dairy Road to South Main Street first, to relieve congestion at the underpass. In 1996, construction was planned to begin in 2000.

The Wake Forest-Rolesville Quiz Bowl team won the state championship in 1998. Team members were Jonathan Smith, Tom Humble, Joe Yakamavich, Brian Charville, Bryan Mabie, John Hodge, Ian James, Kathryn Atkinson, and Luke Tully. *Courtesy of* The Forester, *the Wake Forest-Rolesville High School yearbook*

Wake County had purchased the 13-acre site south of the post office for the library, and the town deeded the old library, valued at $86,000, to help with the costs, which were well over budget. Construction was complete in 1996.

The county also received $53,000 for the library from Henry Love Miller's will. Miller, who lived up to his middle name, died in 1991 after a lifetime of service to his adopted town. A Texan, he came to Wake Forest in 1924, began working in a local automobile repair business, and by 1940 was able to purchase the local Ford dealership on South White Street. In 1945, he purchased a local oil dealership and later sold the car dealership. He was a three-term mayor, a member of the board and chairman of Wake Forest Federal Savings & Loan, and director and head of the Chamber of Commerce. He donated the land for the hospital, and the park along South Franklin Street is named in his honor.

In 2000, after his wife, Angie, died, a trust Miller had set up was distributed. The gifts were $47,000 to the Wake Forest Library, $47,000 to the Trentini Foundation, $25,000 to the Wake Forest Fire Department, $12,500 to Rolesville EMS, and $12,500 to Wake County EMS.

There was a portent of the changing economic times in June when officials at the Burlington Wake Plant announced it would close by the end of the summer, throwing 730-plus employees out of work. It had been one of the principal area employers since 1948.

In mid-summer also, the town commissioners rejected the seminary's second request to rezone land on Capital Boulevard for a shopping center.

And then along came Hurricane Fran. During the wind-filled, tumultuous night of September 5th and 6th, Police Chief Greg Harrington, 10 policemen, and two dispatchers along with every paid and volunteer fireman patrolled all night to check on homes where trees had fallen and to clear what streets they could. Wake Forest residents who had not been jolted out of bed by trees falling on their homes awoke to devastation. The 80-mile-per-hour winds and nine inches of rain combined with ground already saturated from an earlier storm meant trees of every size toppled over. A third of the houses in town suffered serious damage, and trees and downed power and phone lines littered every street. There was no power in town; all of Wake Electric's 18,000 members were without power.

Electric crews and trucks from across the southeast poured into town and the area to help rebuild the broken poles and lines. Two weeks after the storm, all but 180 of Wake

Hurricane Fran blasted through Wake Forest in September of 1996, downing trees and damaging buildings. Julie and Louis Arthur's Victorian home on North Main was one of the hardest hit. *Courtesy of Louis and Julie Arthur*

Electric's customers were back on line, and the only town electric customer who was power-less was the president of Wake Electric, Jim Mangum, who lived in a wooded area off Durham Road.

Total damage to property in town was estimated at $17 million.

Tommy Putnam, a lineman with the town's electric department, was just one of an army of Wake Forest people who turned out to help their neighbors and families recover from the devastation. Although there was a tree down on his house, Putnam moved to his mother's house and worked two-and-a-half weeks repairing power lines before fixing his own. "The stuff I lost was just a drop in the bucket," he said later. "These other people lost some beautiful homes. What I was doing was just some way to help these people get their homes back together. I didn't mind working for the people of Wake Forest because they paid my salary. If it weren't for the people of Wake Forest, I wouldn't be the person I am today. They've always bent over backwards for me."

Former Mayor Tommy Byrne Sr. celebrated his 80th birthday on New Year's Eve 1999. Among those who joined in congratulating him were the then-current Mayor George Mackie and two former mayors, Jimmy Perry and John Lyon.
Courtesy of The Wake Weekly

The U.S. Army Corps of Engineers established a burning and mulching operation at Gresham Lake where bulldozers crawled over a mountain of mulch. For months, every road and highway was littered with the limbs that had fallen off the trucks collecting all the branches and tree trunks.

Sprint, formerly Carolina Telephone, said it would eliminate about a third of the jobs at the headquarters north of town because new technology made it possible to complete financial transaction by telephone.

Dr. I. Beverly Lake Sr. died that year at the age of 90, but not before he had married Kathleen Mackie (both of them were widowed) and administered the oath of office to his son, I. Beverly Jr., as he became an associate justice on the North Carolina Supreme Court in 1992. The older Lake had been a justice there from 1965 until he retired in 1978.

Until this time, candidates in town elections had not really campaigned as we know it today. People knew who they were, and the candidates relied on word of mouth and a few yard signs, if any. The election of 1997 changed that.

The candidates for mayor were Commissioner Bob Hill and George Mackie Jr. It was the first high-dollar campaign, with Mackie, who was successful, spending $14,011 and Hill spending $6,161. Among other things, Mackie accused Hill of belonging to a political clique that controlled town government.

The seminary was deeply involved in the election. Doug Nalley, a former student and the head of the seminary's housing office, always said he was acting as a private citizen, but when President Paige Patterson was asked who the seminary was supporting, he referred the questioner to Nalley. In the 1997 campaign and in others, Nalley encouraged students to register to vote locally, a message echoed in chapel programs. In 1997, Nalley endorsed Hill along with two other candidates, Thomas Walters, the owner of an insurance agency, and Boyce Medlin, a retired state employee. Both were elected.

Meanwhile, the town continued to grow. Almost 300 new homes were permitted in 1997; the Ligon Mill Business Center on South Main Street was about to open; Kenny Geotze and Mark Thompson of Brassfield Realty purchased six buildings in downtown and began renovating and leasing space in them; and James Warren and his law office partners Mike Perry and Sue Anthony broke ground in downtown for a new building. Winn-Dixie, which had been one of the anchors for the Wake Forest Plaza, the town's first shopping center, was about to move to its new building on Durham Road.

Mackie began questioning the seminary's tax-exempt status—something that was questionable once the seminary began asking for rezoning for a shopping center— before he was elected, and he continued to criticize and question the seminary and President Patterson.

But that was just one of the controversies Mackie instigated. He quarreled with all five commissioners. He said the police chief should be fired. He said Town Manager Mark Williams was "in over his head," and he criticized town attorney Eric Vernon.

One of the brighter parts of 1998 was the attention to the DuBois campus. Several schemes to use it had been proposed in the past, but now the National DuBois High School Alumni Association and the DuBois Charter School group headed by Bob Luddy from Youngsville were in a bidding contest to purchase it from the Wake County Board of Education.

For various reasons Luddy dropped out of the bidding in April and found a site on South Franklin Street where he established the charter school, which was renamed Franklin Academy.

In 1994, DuBois alumni celebrated the listing of the W. E. B. DuBois campus on the National Register of Historic Places by holding hands and singing "Hail to Thee DuBois." Pictured are T. J. Culler, Sula Arrington, Harold Winston, Fredrick Jeffreys, William Perry, Minnie Watkins, and Willie Arrington. *Courtesy of* The Wake Weekly

The alumni had raised $65,000 for the down payment and readily agreed to a contract to pay the remaining $260,000 over the next ten years. Their plans were to renovate the buildings, which were showing the neglect since 1989, into a community center where there would be an after-school tutoring program, a computer lab, job

It was an exciting time in town when quintuplets were born to Nancy and Kent Miller on July 7, 1998. Here the three-year-old quints, Grace, Ellie, Emery, Maggie, and Martin, pose with big sister Anna. *Photograph by Charles Garvey, courtesy of the Miller family*

training, adult education classes, and a museum for exhibits about the town's history. The town agreed to spend $100,000 for the necessary work on the gym.

The problems at Northern Wake Rescue and EMS had proven to be so intractable that the directors finally asked the county to take full responsibility for this area. Wake County EMS agreed to build a station and staff it with two ambulances, and Northern Wake was dissolved in 1998. Rolesville EMS, part of the larger group, still continues to serve the town and larger area.

The Business and Industrial Partnership had been formed in 1994, and in 1998 they purchased a large tract off Burlington Mills Road from the Kitchin family, borrowed $286,000 from the town for the site development work, and set out to create South Forest Business Park. BIP has since repaid the full amount to the town, plus $40,000 they had in a never-used contingency account.

Ever since it was built in the 1950s, Wake Forest folks had eaten meals at the seminary cafeteria on Wingate across from the campus, held their club meetings there, and used it for the large gatherings such as the Community Christmas Dinner. There was great dismay when in December 1998 the seminary announced it would close the cafeteria. Karen and Don Winstead, who had operated the cafeteria for 18 years, almost immediately announced they were buying the former Keith's Super Market on Brooks Street and would open a cafeteria there.

The 1999 DOT plan said it would be 2003 before bypass construction would begin.

For at least two years there had been several people urging the town board to adopt voting districts, and in 1999 proponents and opponents voiced sharp differences during another public hearing. Later, the commissioners did not make a decision but instead called for a referendum. By a margin of 1,245 to 480, town voters rejected voting districts.

The spring of 1999 saw further charges from Mayor Mackie, who called on the town board to investigate the police department. The commissioners lashed back, defending the police department and calling Mackie's request dirty politics. A week later, Town Manager Mark Williams released a three-page memo, countering Mackie's claims about the department.

At the 1999 dedication of the Wake Forest Police memorial, Hope Newsom, wife of former Wake Forest Police Chief Harvey Newsom, presented a plaque to family representatives of police officers who died in the line of duty: Cecil Enlow, George Mitchell, and John Taylor. *Courtesy of Jill Bright*

The continuing controversy drew another record number of candidates for the town board.

The decade ended with the town about to turn a new page in growth and governance. Andy Ammons had already received approval for his 944-acre development on the old Marshall-Stroud Dairy land.

While the newly elected commissioners Velma Boyd, Vivian Jones, and Kim Marshall waited in the audience to be sworn in, outgoing commissioners Bob Hill, Al Hinton, and Dan Heimbach, and the two commissioners with two years left on their terms, Thomas Walters and Boyce Medlin, agreed to provide Ammons' Heritage Wake Forest with the water he had requested, 100,000 gallons a day by December 31, 2000, and an additional 100,000 gallons daily each year through December 31, 2003. Mayor Mackie agreed with that, saying, "We fiddled away Wakefield."

The Ruth Snyder Garden at the Wake Forest College Birthplace was dedicated in 1998 on her 92nd birthday.
Artist: Judith Pixton

10

2000–2008

There were new faces in the grocery store—new grocery stores, come to think of it—and new people reinvigorating Wake Forest clubs and churches.

By 2000, the town was seeing the result of those 4,000-plus single-family homes, townhouses, and apartments approved during the 1990s, and there was no sign the growth would stop then or now.

Consider, when 2000 began, there were 12,588 people in town. By the end of the year there were 14,288. Planning Director Chip Russell estimates our town will have 28,860 by the end of 2009.

At the beginning of 2000, about 67 people moved into Wake County each day. That daily stream had increased to an average of 106 new residents each day between July of 2006 and July of 2007. Some of them chose Wake Forest.

Also, there were 5,125 homes as we began the decade, and that number should reach 11,755 before we get to 2010. The town's area will grow from 10.38 square miles in 2000 to 15.91 by 2010, and the miles of streets and roads in town will nearly double, from 36.23 to 72, Director of Engineering Eric Keravuori estimates.

With growth came the need for water. That search for an adequate supply of water for Wake Forest's residents took six years and was a consuming problem for the town's leaders. We will describe it first before we discuss the rest of the decade.

It was not just the town. Wake County officials realized the need for more water and began purchasing land for the Little River reservoir. After a land-use study, the county leaders also recognized that water and sewer services needed to be examined

Everyone present, more than 200 town and county officials as well as town employees and town residents, had a chance to help with the groundbreaking for the new town hall due to open late in 2009. *Courtesy of The Wake Weekly*

and set up a task force which included Wake Forest businessman Don Stroud. The result was a recommendation, without a plan to accomplish it, for a countywide unified utility system. The first step would be two systems, one headed by Raleigh and the other by Cary.

In May 1999, Roe O'Donnell, then the public works and utilities director, told the Wake Forest commissioners the town would need more water by 2003. Town Manager Mark Williams recommended buying an additional one million gallons from Raleigh. (Wake Forest has been purchasing water from Raleigh since 1980 through a line along Capital Boulevard.) The town was already eyeing the intake on the Neuse River at the former Burlington Mills plant as the best way to add to the water it could take from the Smith Creek reservoir.

When Williams approached then-Raleigh City Manager Dempsey Benton about purchasing the million gallons, Benton told him the city wanted to slow growth in the smaller towns and could not continue to support the towns' growth. Benton did agree to sell the town another 360,000 gallons a day at once and 440,000 gallons later, but that additional water would have to be renegotiated if the town won state approval for the Neuse intake.

The steeple of Binkley Chapel on the Southeastern Seminary campus is a familiar beacon to people entering Wake Forest from the east or the west. In this painting of Roosevelt Street, the underpass is in the center and the white building on the right is the old bus station, now a car repair business.
Artist: Ed Hardy

Those first steps set the framework for the water quest. Raleigh's concern was that the intake would require a water-supply watershed that would cover the developing Falls River and Wakefield subdivisions and might restrict commercial development along the Capital Boulevard corridor, a fear that was shared by some local developers.

With board approval, Commissioner Thomas Walters set up a small task force in 2000. "Our vision was a regional water system," Walters said, one in which all participants would have a voice. Despite opposition from developers and Southeastern Baptist Theological Seminary, the state Environmental Management Commission agreed to Wake Forest's request to reclassify the Neuse intake and its watershed as a drinking water source in October 2000.

At about this time Benton and his successors Carolyn Carter and Russell Allen began to pressure the town to defer the Neuse reclassification and to begin negotiating to merge its water and sewer with Raleigh based on the model used for the Rolesville and Garner takeovers, in which the towns brought little or nothing to the table.

Wake Forest also looked at other water sources. One was Kerr Lake, where Henderson controlled the sole intake. Henderson was not interested in selling water to the town. It would have been costly to build the lines from Louisburg, another possibility, and its water source, the Tar River, can have a very low flow in the summer.

Cost was a factor. Wake Forest had high water and sewer rates, compared to other nearby municipalities, because it had invested heavily in its systems.

Raleigh gave Wake Forest officials a draft of a water and sewer merger agreement early in 2002, and an informal survey showed that most town residents preferred lower rates over maintaining an independent utility system.

That summer there was a lot of negative publicity about the Raleigh water treatment plant and the water it produced. In September, George Rogers, the town's water resources superintendent, was ready to shut down the Raleigh water main and order water plant operators to open fire hydrants and dump Raleigh water if it had less than the required chlorine.

The commissioners had agreed to begin negotiations about a merger with Raleigh, but they were also authorizing studies about the costs of merger and about the costs of remaining independent and pulling six to 10 million gallons a day from the Neuse. They began holding closed-door sessions with John Elmore and John Lancaster, two of the owners of the old Burlington plant.

Most of the town residents who went to the public meeting in October 2003 wanted to keep the town's system. Peggy Allen, the retired *Wake Weekly* editor, said, "We're not going to have any control over the growth of Wake Forest. Water is the most important thing we have."

The fall of 2003 was critical. An interim water contract with Raleigh would end in 2007. If the town wished to remain independent it had to begin work immediately in order to have the upgraded intake, the large new water line, and the expanded water treatment plant completed by then. The cost was estimated at $20 million.

Commissioner Chris Malone said he wanted to continue the dual track, negotiating with Raleigh and also paying the engineering firm of Hazen & Sawyer $300,000 to design the intake, line, and plant expansion. The board voted to do so.

Two weeks later, a new study said the cost of merger with Raleigh would be higher

The Chamber of Commerce's Leadership Wake Forest program was developed to encourage community involvement, and the 2005 class made service a primary focus of their experience. Shown here with food, school supplies, and money collected for the DuBois Center are, from left, Erica Braman, Adrian Bridges, Tony Compione, Michael Siderio, Jeff Adolphsen, Richard Hamilton, Angelo Pettis, Chris Kaeberlein, Jonathan Hand, Jim Staples, Bill Crabtree, Michael Massey, and Wendy Anderson. *Courtesy of the Wake Forest Chamber of Commerce*

A group celebrated the 2004 Christmas season with a get-together in the craft room of the Northern Wake Senior Center. *Courtesy of the Northern Wake Senior Center*

than thought at first—$17 million against the original $10 million—and there would be less water—8.6 million gallons a day in 2025 as opposed to the 10 to 12 million gallons a day possible from the intake. The numbers for the Neuse River intake changed with every study.

By this time the town board had agreed on several goals for their negotiations with Raleigh, including a voice in the operations of the merged system, autonomy about growth decisions, value for the town's excellent water and sewer systems, and a start toward a countywide system.

When the two negotiating teams met in November 2003, Raleigh's team was more than "somewhat surprised," as Town Manager Mark Williams later told a Chamber of Commerce committee, because the town's negotiators came armed with their goals for the merger. Raleigh Mayor Charles Meeker, City Manager Russell Allen, and other staff members had been prepared to settle the fine details of merger. They were so startled by the town's position they had to excuse themselves and leave the room momentarily to regain their composure.

It was January 2004 before Allen responded, sending a letter to Williams that made no concessions to the town's goals but did express concern about the reclassification of the Neuse River for drinking water. He wanted to conclude the merger agreement by July 1.

One of the most troublesome questions, never resolved, that the Wake Forest board faced during talks about merger was how fast the town would grow. The proposed merger agreement said the town would grow by 8 percent in each of the first two years of merger, then drop back to 4 percent growth.

Wake Forest had grown by 10 percent each of the previous years, Mayor Vivian Jones said in May, and approved subdivisions would mean an equal increase in 2004 and beyond. Some commissioners—and eventually all of them—agreed the town would be best served by vigorous growth, 800 new homes each year, to pay off the merger cost faster.

Raleigh had been insisting on a 10-year merger transition period during which the city would profit by as much as $25 million. In February, however, city officials agreed the transition for Wake Forest could be shorter, four to five years. The Wake Forest Town Board responded by voting to begin merger implementation—without agreeing to a contract—but they asked that there be no transition period.

A young couple enjoys a summer day at the Smith Creek reservoir which provided some of Wake Forest's water until the town merged its water and sewer system with Raleigh in 2005. *Artist: Dan Russell*

In July, Planning Director Chip Russell began assembling and publishing a spreadsheet he continues to update monthly, listing all the approved subdivisions and the number of lots in each that remain to be built. There were 10,127 lots, and at a conservative 2.2 residents per house, those new homes would add 22,279 people. Russell estimated 951 homes would be built in 2004.

At the same time, Deputy Town Manager Roe O'Donnell said the town would grow by 8 percent through the end of 2005 and then slow to 4 percent and would not need more than 4.71 million gallons of water a day for the first five years of merger.

Another factor emerged in 2004. With a rapidly growing population, Wake Forest needed street improvements and parks. To pay for them, the town planned to ask voters to approve two bond issues, bonds which would sizably increase the town's debt. The state, through the Local Government Commission, closely watches every town's debt to make sure it is not overextended. The LGC might not approve bonds for streets and parks if the town was also using bonds to finance the $20 to $25 million for the Neuse water improvements.

September of 2004 saw two seminal events, connected because they showed the direction in which the commissioners were leaning. Early in the month they began discussing the possible projects for bond referendums in the spring. At the regular board meeting, Commissioners Stephen Barrington, Rob Bridges, and Chris Malone voted not to spend $100,000 for the design of the Neuse River water intake and the water treatment plant expansion. "If moving ahead with the bonds means going with

Jazz Festival Poster *Courtesy of Barbara Massenburg*

Thomas Taylor, left, and Ira Tripp practice on the drums during the third annual DuBois Jazz Festival in 2002. Ira, then a fifth-grader at Jones Dairy Elementary School, was one of six children and youth who participated in a jazz workshop at the DuBois Center. Some of the state's best-known jazz instructors came to town to share their knowledge with the hope of sparking the next generation of jazz musicians. *Courtesy of* The News & Observer

merger, then I say go ahead with the bonds," Barrington said. The vote was seen as a signal that the town would choose merger.

On November 16, after two lengthy work sessions, the town commissioners unanimously voted for the water/sewer merger with Raleigh, saying maintaining an independent utility system would place too heavy a financial burden on the town customers. That burden would include $25 million to begin using the Neuse River water and a future $15 million in system improvements.

Under merger, which became effective July 1, 2005, the town is paying an estimated $15 million for Raleigh to upgrade the systems, $3 million for an additional one million gallons of water and $710,000 for additional sewer capacity. The town has up to 4.91 million gallons of water on peak days through the spring of 2010.

Although assuring adequate water and sewer was the most momentous discussion and decision of this decade, it was only one of many decisions and events.

One of the first was the hiring of the town's first economic developer, Stephen Barrington, whose position was paid by town funds and donations from area businesses. Town officials, business leaders, and the Wake Forest Chamber of Commerce board agreed on the need for new industry to augment the industrial jobs at Athey Products, Parker-Hannifin, and Weavexx.

Wake Forest residents had already dealt with three snow storms that January in 2000, but neither they nor their trusted forecasters expected the paralyzing northeaster that dumped 20 inches of snow over two days, January 24th and 25th. The storm shut down everything for days, Town Manager Mark Williams recalls, not just here but across a wide swath in the middle of the state.

The DuBois Center was beginning to offer a variety of activities for children and adults in the nearby community, and the town and its residents were offering help.

The town, besides paying for the water, sewer, and lights, donated $64,000 to renovate the gym. The Wake Forest Cultural Arts Alliance joined with the DuBois alumni and the center's director, Bettie Murchison, to stage the first DuBois Jazz Festival, a social event that continued through 2005.

Andy Ammons was building the roads and installing the

infrastructure for Heritage, and that included changing the Forestville Road-Rogers Road intersection and building a new section of Rogers out to South Main Street.

The new section of Rogers crossed the CSX rail line; the state Department of Transportation and CSX would only agree to the new crossing if the existing Forestville crossing was closed. Doug Walston and others strongly opposed that closing, and many people signed their petitions. They and others protested at a public meeting, but the dangerous crossing in a curve was closed as was the East Sycamore crossing in downtown.

DOT was finally serious about the N.C. 98 bypass, which local leaders had urged for more than 30 years. Early in 2000, Jonathan Nance, head of DOT's District Five, told the town commissioners and members of the Chamber of Commerce that the contracts for the first leg would be let in the spring of 2001 and would be built at the full four lanes rather than the two DOT had proposed at one time. Later in the year, DOT included funding for all three bypass sections in its seven-year construction plan and said construction for the last section would begin in 2008.

Surveys had shown that town residents wanted more parks and greenways. The town was preparing an open space and greenway plan that was adopted in 2002, but in the spring of 2000 the first greenway section, Kiwanis Park between South Franklin

More active elements in the Joyner Farm Park plan are a playground, baseball and soccer fields, and a community center. *Courtesy of the Town of Wake Forest*

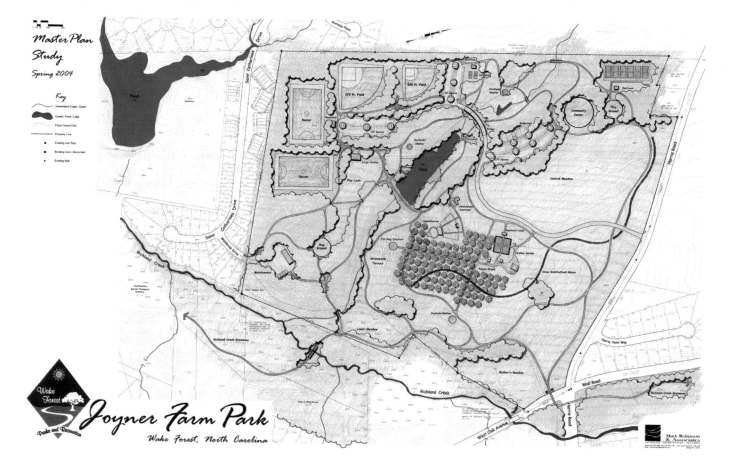

Pete Hendricks and his crew restored farm buildings to their original state for the town's Joyner Park project. The Walker Homestead is one facet of the 117-acre park that includes trails, a pond, pecan groves, an amphitheater, and a performance garden. *Courtesy of The Wake Weekly*

In 2000, the Historic Preservation Commission hosted a tour of gardens on North Main Street. Other clubs joined in and the tour has been continued as a Wake Forest Garden Club project and expanded to include other areas of town. *Courtesy of Agnes Wanman*

Street and South White Street, was opened.

Mayor George Mackie continued to question the town departments and attempted to establish a citizen committee to investigate what he called "discrimination, mismanagement, and intimidation in the police department and other departments." Commissioner Kim Marshall responded with a memo saying such a committee was not approved by the town board and was a part of the mayor's "personal vendetta against the town government and its administration." Commissioner Vivian Jones chastised Mackie, saying, "You have embarrassed the Town of Wake Forest and its citizens."

Wake Foresters have always cherished their heritage and sought to preserve the past, but the impetus for preservation grew through the decades after the college left. At first young couples bought the fine old homes along North Main because they were affordable; then they began to restore them. They and others helped establish the North Main historic district in 1979 with a commission that ensures the homes are preserved.

The Historic Preservation Commission was instrumental in focusing attention on the Royall Mill Village, and in 1999 it was designated as an historic district on the National Register of Historic Places. Next the planning department and the town board turned to the South White Street downtown area, which was placed on the National Register in 2002, and in 2003 the entire historic core of the town was also placed on the National Register.

2000 was the year for the biennial Christmas Tour sponsored by the Wake Forest Historic Preservation Commission, and one of the houses was Cameron Heights, built in 1912 by William Royall Powell, a son of one of the mill's founders, and his wife, Suzy Cameron Lanneau Powell. It was their dream home with maple and pine floors, leaded-glass windows, and even a giant central vacuum. Suzy, an ardent gardener, directed the landscaping of the grounds. During the Depression, when they nearly lost the house, the Powells sectioned off the second floor and rented it to a medical fraternity. When the fraternity left because the college's medical school moved to Winston-Salem, the second floor became a dormitory for the first coeds at the college. After William died in the 1940s, the entire house was cut up into apartments. Bob and Liz Ford purchased the house in 1966 and had been restoring it ever since.

All during 2000, there had been unsettling news from Athey Products, workers laid off and then called back and, once, the work week cut to four days. Then, on the first

Friday in December, the company president told the 130 production workers to go home and apply for unemployment.

Director Mark Fleming and the staff at the Wake Forest Chamber of Commerce quickly organized a drive to help the workers and their families over the holidays, and people in the area responded generously. James Cloonan, a former Athey president, moved into the conference room at *The Wake Weekly* and began helping the former employees, some of whom had been with Athey since it moved to town in 1965, find new jobs.

Six months later, in May 2001, Parker-Hannifin (formerly Schrader) said it would end operations by the end of the year. At one point the plant that made industrial hydraulic parts had employed as many as 650 people, but it had been downsizing and only 140 employees were left.

There was intense interest in the 2001 town election. Mackie said he was not running for a second term because he had plans to run for another office in two years, but two weeks before the election he announced as a write-in candidate because he had been encouraged by a telephone poll. The two announced candidates were Commissioners Vivian Jones and Boyce Medlin, and Jones won by a large margin. Rob Bridges and Chris Malone were elected to the board, joining Commissioners Kim Marshall and Velma Boyd. David Camacho, who came in third in the balloting, was chosen soon after to finish Jones' term as commissioner.

With Heritage underway, Andy Ammons turned his attention to a family-owned, 900-acre tract west of the town reservoir. He submitted plans for a subdivision including school sites and construction of the North Loop. Russell said there were several reasons why the planning department could not tackle the plans at the time, including a lack of staff.

Three Raleigh developers said they had a contract to purchase the Wake Forest Plaza, although only one, Craig Briner acting as East Elm Associates, eventually bought the property, the town's first shopping center, and some adjacent empty land.

Flaherty Community Center was completed, a building that included the first town-owned gymnasium and crafts center. The town had been developing J. B. Flaherty Park since 1993 when it purchased 23 acres for the ball fields. Over the succeeding years, the Flaherty family had donated the rest of the 100 acres where there are now three lighted ball fields, two ponds, eight lighted tennis courts, a playground, and a two-acre dog park.

Mayor Vivian Jones and Parks and Recreation Director Susan Simpson cut the ribbon at the dedication of the Flaherty Park Community Center as Commissioner Chris Malone and Town Manager Mark Williams looked on. *Courtesy of the Wake Weekly*

Town crews installed the new Centennial banners along White Street in time for the 2008 Meet in the Street festival. *Courtesy of the Town of Wake Forest*

Brandon Roper and his cousin Powell Roper sliced some of their homegrown tomatoes to make sandwiches for Saturday morning visitors at the Wake Forest Farmers Market. *Courtesy of* The Wake Weekly

The Lions Gate Inn, the town's first bed and breakfast, opened in 2007. Pictured is the dining room, decorated for the biannual Christmas Tour of Historic Homes. *Courtesy of* In Style *magazine*

Several hundred volunteers, from children to senior citizens, gathered at the Wake Forest Boys and Girls Club to assist the Wake Forest Rotary Club in packaging meals for Stop Hunger Now's Million Meals Project. Wake Forest volunteers packaged 63,938 meals in 2006 and 66,158 meals in 2007. *Photograph by Ryan Keith*

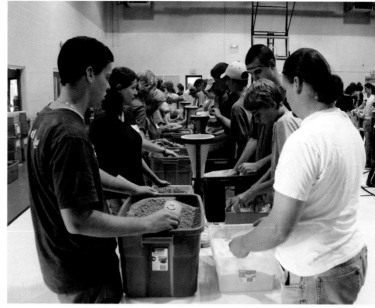

Caps flew into the air at Franklin Academy's first graduation in 2006. The charter school was opened on Franklin Street as an elementary school in 1998 and a high school on Chalks Road was built in 2002. *Courtesy of* The Wake Weekly

Tree-lined North Main Street is a source of pleasure when the maples turn in the fall. *Photograph by Hugh Nourse*

There had been a rainfall deficit since 1998, and the summer of 2002 was exceptionally dry. The Fourth of July fireworks program in Trentini Stadium was threatened, but a timely rain shower allowed the show to go on.

Raleigh enacted mandatory conservation rules that allowed lawn watering only every other day, and Wake Forest, because of its contract with the city, had to have the same rules. The fine for a violation was $500, which was highly unpopular.

A Wal-Mart developer was eyeing the town, leading to a lively public discussion.

Scouting has a long history in Wake Forest. Boy Scout Troop 5 was chartered on February 1, 1931, the fifth in the state, and there are now eight troops and one post in town. In 2007, nine members of Troop 303 achieved Eagle Scout status. They are (back) Will Braddy, Thomas Sizemore, Hayden Montgomery, Spencer Warehime, Keaton Epps, (front) Nathan Weber, Matthew Baker, Cory Winterton, and Abel Salgado. *Courtesy of Scoutmaster Jack Baker*

Mayor Vivian Jones was opposed to the store; public opinion gauged by letters to the editor was heavily in favor. The Aiken, S.C., firm that would build the store had told Planning Director Chip Russell that the favored site was just north of the Weavexx site on South Main Street.

2002 ended with a damaging ice storm on Wednesday, December 4, that downed the power lines for all 6,500 town electric customers and turned out the lights across central North Carolina. A 23-man crew from Greenville, another member of ElectriCities, rolled into town Thursday with 10 trucks. Together with the town crews, they had restored almost all the power by Sunday. Some town residents were still in the dark, though, because they are served by Wake Electric and what was then CP&L.

The year 2003 began with an announcement from Weavexx, the town's last industry. It planned to phase out manufacturing that spring, offer severance benefits and outplacement services to its 133 hourly employees, and close the plant by the end of the year. The manufacturing operations were to be moved to an Ontario, Canada, plant, but the company's corporate headquarters would remain in Wake Forest.

Also in January, the directors for the Wake Forest Fire Department named Jimmy Keith as the department's first paid full-time chief. He took over a department with 36 volunteer firemen, 12 full-time paid, and eight part-time paid firemen. Keith was named the unpaid chief in 1987, and in 1993 the board voted to pay him for his part-time hours. Until 2003, Keith also worked a full-time job, first at the family grocery store which closed in 1993 and then at a grocery store in Raleigh.

Jimmy's grandfather, Frank Keith, was a charter member of the town fire department when it was formed in 1921 and was the chief for 17 years. He also established Keith's Super Market on South White Street. Frank's sons, Bruce and Raymond, were longtime volunteer firemen. Bruce, Jimmy's father, was a department director for several years and the chief for three. Raymond's son, Clifton, is also a volunteer fireman and an assistant fire chief. Finally, Jimmy's brother-in-law, Gary Sullivan is a veteran volunteer firefighter.

Rena Sproston helped the Wake Forest Woman's Club team win the Wake Forest Chamber of Commerce's eleventh annual Spelling Bee. *Courtesy of* The Wake Weekly

Jim Adams and Jim Goldston bought the Athey plant in 2001 and posted a sign saying it was available: "Be creative," they advised would-be buyers. Jeff Ammons, Andy's younger brother and owner of Ammons Builders, took the advice and decided the town needed a place where people could skate, play indoor soccer, work out, shop, and eat—The Factory, which opened in 2004.

Then he looked at the back 40 acres and thought "ball fields." He set up a nonprofit foundation to own the ball fields and lease them for tournament play, and then, with the backing of town officials and the Chamber of Commerce, Ammons applied for and received $1.5 million of the county's hotel and food taxes to build the fields. Capital City Baseball schedules and operates the youth baseball tournaments.

In 2003, the seminary was no longer a factor in town elections. President Paige Patterson had resigned to take another position, and in October Doug Nalley confirmed he would no longer be endorsing town board candidates and standing at the door of the polling place most students used, urging them to vote for his slate. There were only four candidates for the three open seats; Stephen Barrington, Velma Boyd, and David Camacho were elected.

All during these years, the town board was continuing to add people, homes, and land without a plan for the necessary water. In February 2004 Mayor Vivian Jones asked, "Do we want to continue to accept these petitions for annexation before we decide what we're going to do about water?" None of the commissioners responded. Between June 2003 and March 2004 the town board annexed 1,286 acres that became, among other uses, the Margot's Pond, Bishop's Grant, Heritage South, and Wildflower subdivisions and the Lowe's Home Improvements Store.

Since the 1930s, the Underpass had been the town's billboard, the place where the firemen hung banners announcing their fish fries, where churches told everyone about their fall barbecue dinners and bazaars, and where the Chamber of Commerce banners advertised the Christmas parade.

But that simpler, more trusting era ended in March 2004 when CSX Railroad announced it would no longer allow banners on the underpass bridge because of heightened concerns about security after 9/11 and because rock-throwing vandals had been hiding behind the banners, breaking windows and causing damage all along Roosevelt Avenue.

2004 will be remembered as the year when it seemed every street in town was torn up or under construction of some kind. South Main Street was being widened to five lanes in piecemeal fashion while the town negotiated with DOT for funding to complete the project; Barnhill Contracting was finishing the first leg of the bypass, and there was a temporary detour on South Main Street while dump trucks brought in enough dirt to raise the street by 12 feet for an at-grade crossing with the bypass; Barnhill was also building the extension of South Franklin Street from a dead-end to the bypass; S. T. Wooten was clearing the right-of-way for the second bypass leg; and another contractor had closed Stadium Drive in order to rebuild the bridge over Richland Creek.

When the second leg of the N.C. 98 bypass was being built over Capital Boulevard, a conveyor belt designed by S. T. Wooten Corporation was used to carry soil and rock to fill a depression on the western side without interrupting the flow of traffic below. *Courtesy of* The Wake Weekly

People drove—cautiously—and walked to a temporary office in the old Wake Forest Plaza to tell consultants what they wanted to see in downtown in 10 or 20 years. The result became the Renaissance Plan, which covers the heart of the town and provides a context for public and private investment.

The Sunflower Studio and Gallery is one of the anchors of downtown's Art After Hours held the second Friday night of each month. *Artist: Linda Burrell*

At the beginning of June 2004, Margaret Jones Stinnett announced the last of the longtime Wake Forest businesses, Jones Hardware, would close June 30 because of competition from Home Depot and because a traffic island blocked left turns into its site on Durham Road. Stinnett sold the South White Street store in 1991 and moved to Durham Road. The Durham Road land now houses a Walgreen's drugstore.

Her grandfather, I. O. Jones, founded Wake Forest Supply Company in 1906 in a brick building on the corner of South White and Jones Avenue. In 1916, he completed a new building on the west side of the street and sold the old one to T. E. Holding for his drugstore. Leland Jones joined his father in 1931 and the name was changed to Jones Hardware in 1935. Leland ran the store with veteran employees George Timberlake and Bill Shearon.

The entire town was saddened and hundreds turned out to mourn when Fire Chief Jimmy Keith died of cancer in August.

Construction of the "hill" on South Main was completed and the first section of the bypass opened in August.

Commissioners Barrington, Bridges, and Malone were the three votes for two controversial projects. One was for 63 townhomes on Durham Road that would be built partly in the Richland Creek floodplain, and the second was the Shoppes at Caveness Farm, a shopping center the planning board had voted seven to three against recommending. Neither was built.

The downtown was experiencing another of its cyclical convulsions in the winter of 2004; altogether nine stores had left or planned to close shortly. At the same time, the town and the Downtown Revitalization Corporation received a state Department of Transportation grant of $84,856 to do a survey and hire a design firm to plan how to replace the curb, gutter, and sidewalks on two blocks of South White Street. The town committed $197,991 toward the project.

The end-of-year news was that the Wake County Board of Education had approved a lease with the DuBois Center for a temporary modular school and had purchased a 20-acre site in Wakefield for the future Forest Pines Elementary School.

It turned out that the town's residential growth in 2004 was even larger than Russell had anticipated. The town issued 1,116 residential building permits, a 15 percent increase in the town's homes.

As soon as the assignment plan for the modular school was released in 2005, a number of Wakefield parents began organizing a protest that turned very ugly. A local television station ran a clip in which one parent complained, "You are going to move people from Wakefield to the slums of Wake Forest." Wake Forest residents were incensed, agreeing with Mayor Jones, who said, "Wake Forest has no slums. We are proud of everyone in our community. We support the DuBois Center." They also agreed with Mary Evelyn Jones, who said "We deserve an apology for the way our community has been belittled and lied on."

The protesting parents made headlines through the spring and summer, finally suing the school board, a suit that was dismissed by Superior Court Judge Wade Barber Jr. in early August. Halfway through the school year the parents whose children were in the modular school were saying it was a fine school and expressing their satisfaction.

Most town voters must have been satisfied, because they stayed home and let 363 out of the 433 who turned up at the polls in May approve the $16.5 million in bonds for parks, streets, and sidewalks. It was mostly state money paying for the final widening and paving of South Main between Capital Boulevard and Rogers Road.

Although the roof was gone and the brick walls were standing with supports, the DuBois Center director, Bettie Murchison, saw a renovated gleaming building in the future, a building that would be the National Rosenwald School Museum. On a windy day in March 2005, she and the board members for the National DuBois High School Alumni Association kicked off a $3 million capital campaign that was backed by Julius Rosenwald's grandchildren and supported by three congressmen and several other state and local officials.

The Veterans Memorial at Heritage Wake Forest was dedicated Sunday, November 11, 2001, ending a three-year effort by area veterans and volunteers. Here some volunteers are assembling the impressive monument. The Stony Hill Veterans Memorial was dedicated the same day.
Courtesy of Jill Bright

Mayor Jones effectively stifled any possible opposition by announcing early for a second term. In November, Frank Drake and Margaret Stinnett, who both told voters they were concerned about the town's explosive growth, won seats on the town board, ousting incumbents Bridges and Malone.

There was some obvious but muted discord among the directors for the Wake Forest Fire Department. David Williams Jr., who had been named first interim chief and then full-time chief after Jimmy Keith's death, agreed to step down because, as head of his own construction company, he kept irregular hours at the fire station. The directors and Williams were united, though, when they presented the need for a third fire station, one on the west side of town, to the town commissioners. Developer Jim Adams promised he would set aside land near Kearney and Wake Union Church roads. Town Manager Mark Williams said the $1.32-million station would probably mean another 3 cents on the tax rate.

During 2005, while commissioners discussed growth limits, the town issued 1,005 permits for residences. At the January 2006 town board retreat, Planning Director

The Wake Forest Titans, 12 to 14 years old, were the winners of the 2007 Pop Warner Junior Midget National championship tournament in Orlando, Florida.
Courtesy of Anthony Cascio

Russell told the commissioners the town would not need more water than the 4.91 million gallons a day agreed on in the merger if they built no more than 3,200 homes in the next four years, or 800 a year. The town's water allotment will increase in the spring of 2010.

With the Renaissance Plan setting out a blueprint for the heart of the town, with a streetscape plan underway for South White Street, with the bypass assured of completion, Franklin Street linked to the bypass, with voter approval for parks and streets, and with South Main finally completely widened and paved, the commissioners turned to another area that had been overlooked, the northeast quadrant, also called the East End and the DuBois Community. They hired a consultant to study it.

They also hired a consultant for a new land-use plan or, in this case, a community plan.

Trouble had also been brewing at the DuBois Center, and early in 2006 Bettie Murchison resigned as director, saying the alumni association president, her cousin Lawrence Eugene Perry, and other board members wanted to focus on other projects than the social programs she had begun at the center.

Joel R. Young, the owner of the Wake Forest Golf Club, disturbed his neighbors, most of whom had bought or built their houses to be near or on a golf course, by announcing he would sell the course to Centex Homes for development as a subdivision, a deal that fell through.

A new town hall had been a goal for years, and now the question was where to build it. The Renaissance Plan envisioned a town green and town hall somewhere along Elm Avenue, and the possible sites had been narrowed to two, the DAB site near the old Wake Forest Plaza and Brooks Street. During a public meeting, most speakers favored the DAB site. Developer Craig Briner promised to build Brooks through to East Holding, refurbish the plaza buildings, build a three-story office building at Brooks and Elm and bring the town a site plan for 120 upscale townhomes if the choice was the DAB site.

The town commissioners, who would grow increasingly aware of the need to manage the available water, agreed in March to limit the number of building permits a subdivision could have in a year to 40. The number had been set at 50 per year in 2001.

At that same meeting, Deputy Town Manager Roe O'Donnell revealed a glaring problem with the merger water projections—the new residents were using much more water because the builders and the homeowners were installing irrigation systems. "We wanted to show you that at the time of merger, our data was accurate. What has changed is our usage patterns have changed dramatically the past few years," Town Manager Mark Williams said.

The very next developers seeking approval for a residential development were former Fire Chief David Williams Jr. and his partners Steve and David Faircloth, who are not related. They arrived at the town board's comprehensive planning committee with a list of 100 ways to conserve water and agreed to install water-saving appliances, plant drought-resistant shrubs, trees, and grass, and not to use town water for irrigation.

By April, the drought that had hit the Triangle almost every summer since 1998 was severe, and Raleigh mandated strict water conservation measures.

The second leg of the bypass, from South Main Street to Capital Boulevard, opened in June.

The U.S. Census confirmed what many people knew or sensed. It said Rolesville and Wake Forest grew the fastest, in terms of percent, of any towns in North Carolina. Between July 1, 2004, and July 1, 2005, Rolesville grew by 19.3 percent and Wake Forest by 14.7 percent. The numbers were smaller in Rolesville; it grew from 1,038 people in 2004 to 1,238 in 2005. But Wake Forest added 2,576 residents, growing from 17,550 to 20,126. The Wake Forest Planning Department, however, said there were 20,300 people in town by the end of 2004.

The industrial conversion was nearly complete. Athey had become The Factory. Glenn Boyd purchased the former Weavexx property for $5.6 million—it had been listed at $6.1 million—and was grinding up the buildings to fill a gully and level the land for a car dealership. And Jim Adams, who had been negotiating for three years, finally purchased the old Parker-Hannifin plant and 30 acres for $2.9 million. He planned a major shopping center there.

That summer of 2006 the town board agreed on the Brooks Street site for the new town hall.

Early in the fall, Lib Perry and Bill Andrews, members of the Holding family, announced they would develop their half of the former dairy farm as Holding Village. Their partner would be Roger Perry, who built Meadowmont in Chapel Hill, and their goal was a walkable, mixed-use neighborhood much like Wake Forest's downtown once was. They planned about 1,300 homes. Within six weeks, the town board agreed to allocate water, expressed in building permits, for the project: 100 in 2007, 200 in 2008 and every year thereafter until build-out, as well as 260 apartments in any year.

The fire department had gone outside the department for the first time in selecting a chief and hired Jerry Swift from Gastonia. He hit the ground at a gallop and by fall was telling the town board it would take $16 million to build, equip, and staff the three new fire stations that were needed as soon as possible to cut the response time to five minutes to reach every occupied building in town. There was extra attention to the fire department because fires had destroyed three large homes in the large-lot subdivisions along Thompson Mill Road where there were no fire hydrants. That area is in the Falls Lake watershed controlled by Wake County zoning, which calls for lots of at least an acre.

The 906 building permits in 2006 were still more than the 800 the commissioners wanted, but were fewer than in the past two years. The town's estimated population was 22,784.

The community meetings for the Northeast Plan were going well because the residents were being very vocal, saying they had close ties to the area and wanted to continue to live there, but they wanted more services, particularly a grocery store, and better streets, sidewalks, street lights, and housing.

In 2007, the town finally had its first bed and breakfast, having turned down four applications in the past. Bill and Louise Howard had restored the Reid house on

A large crowd gathered on the grounds of the Wake Forest College Birthplace for a concert featuring David LaMotte, the son of a former Wake Forest Presbyterian Church minister. The popular Six Sundays in Spring concert series sponsored by the Wake Forest Cultural Arts Association began in 1994. *Courtesy of* The Wake Weekly

Some of the town's treasured trees.
Photograph by Agnes Wanman

North Main Street, and Al Dubber, the most vocal opponent to three of the requests, spoke in favor of the Howards' request. "They have turned a Volkswagen junkyard into a beautiful, elegant house."

As cloudless skies continued during the summer, as Wake County was labeled as experiencing exceptional drought, the most severe designation, and as Falls Lake turned into an expanse of mud flats, the Wake Forest commissioners and mayor became increasingly concerned and proactive about water conservation, approving a policy that "strongly discourages" the use of treated water for irrigation. They also sent letters to the City of Raleigh urging stronger, faster water conservation across the system.

There were two preservation efforts that summer. Mayor Jones and several others had been fretting because the historic South Brick House was for sale and they feared it would be torn down. Instead, a young couple with local ties, Jim and Alexis Cooke, purchased it for their home. A second house that was architecturally significant and had ties to the Lake family stood in the footprint for the new Patterson Hall on the seminary campus. Capital Area Preservation, Kathryn and Frank Drake, and the seminary finagled, plotted, and finally were able to save the house by cutting it in half for the move to a new site on North College Street.

Centex had backed out of the earlier plan to develop the Wake Forest Golf Club, but in October owner Joel Young announced another plan to sell the golf course. This time the affected neighbors took the matter to court but have since withdrawn their suit.

After a lively campaign, Wake Forest voters elected three slow-growth or sensible-growth candidates to the town board: Anne Hines, Chris Kaeberlein, and Peter Thibodeau.

One of the factors in the election had to be the vision for the town that developed from two community meetings where people said they wanted greenways, parks, recreation opportunities, a vibrant downtown, lower taxes, retention of the small-town character, and well-planned infrastructure, among other things. The steering committee for the Community Plan continued to meet through the first part of 2008, assembling the policies to achieve the goals set out in the meetings.

Wake County dedicated the new Northern Regional Center in January, a facility that brought almost every county service to the area.

The plans for the new town hall were finalized, and the groundbreaking was held in May with promises that it will be complete for the final centennial event in December 2009.

Mayor Vivian Jones achieved one of her goals in April when she announced that a coalition of the town, Triangle Transit, Raleigh's CAT system, and the county's TRACS program would provide express commuter buses to and from Raleigh and a local bus inside town.

By a three-to-two vote, with Commissioners Hines, Kaeberlein, and Thibodeau voting yes, the town approved what may be the last large mixed-use development, Traditions, planned by the Ammons family.

By a unanimous vote, the commissioners agreed to protect the town's water allocation and prohibit connecting irrigation systems to the treated water system.

And so we end this incomplete story about our town's most recent century, ending as we began—in the middle. Momentous changes were underway when we picked up the story; we know momentous changes are underway today. Y'all stay around and see what happens.

appendix

Mayors and Board Members of the Town of Wake Forest

5-03-1909
MAYOR: J. C. Caddell
BOARD OF COMMISSIONERS: F. W. Dickson, C. E. Brewer, C. E. Gill,
Z. V. Peed, W. B. Dunn Jr.

11-28-1910
Commissioner Peed offered his resignation and it was accepted. Prof.
J. B. Carlyle was elected to fill the vacancy.

5-04-1911
MAYOR: J. C. Caddell
BOARD OF COMMISSIONERS: F. W. Dickson, O. K. Holding, C. E. Gill,
W. E. Mitchell, C. E. Brewer

5-05-1913
MAYOR: J. C. Caddell
BOARD OF COMMISSIONERS: C. E. Brewer, C. E. Gill, F. W. Dickson,
W. E. Mitchell, W. R. Powell

5-03-1915
MAYOR: J. C. Caddell
BOARD OF COMMISSIONERS: F. W. Dickson, W. R. Powell, W. E. Mitchell,
J. M. Brewer, E. W. Timberlake Jr.

5-08-1917
MAYOR: J. G. Mills
BOARD OF COMMISSIONERS: F. W. Dickson, W. R. Powell, J. M. Brewer,
E. W. Timberlake Jr., R. H. Mitchell

11-07-1918
I. O. Jones unanimously elected commissioner to fill vacancy caused by
the death of Commissioner R. H. Mitchell

5-05-1919
MAYOR: J. G. Mills
BOARD OF COMMISSIONERS: F. W. Dickson, J. M. Brewer, W. R. Powell,
E. W. Timberlake Jr., I. O. Jones

05-02-1921
MAYOR: J. G. Mills
BOARD OF COMMISSIONERS: J. M. Brewer, F. W. Dickson, I. O. Jones,
W. R. Powell, E. W. Timberlake Jr.

5-08-1923
MAYOR: J. G. Mills
BOARD OF COMMISSIONERS: J. M. Brewer, F. W. Dickson, I. O. Jones,
W. R. Powell, E. W. Timberlake Jr.

1-08-1925
The resignation of Mayor J. G. Mills offered January 1, 1925, was
accepted. A. J. Davis was unanimously elected mayor to fill the unexpired
term of former Mayor J. G. Mills.

4-03-1925
The resignation of Commissioner J. M. Brewer was accepted. Dr. J. H.
Gorrell was elected to fill unexpired term of Commissioner J. M. Brewer.

5-05-1925
MAYOR: A. J. Davis
BOARD OF COMMISSIONERS: F. W. Dickson, J. H. Gorrell, W. R. Powell,
E. W. Timberlake Jr., R. W. Wilkinson

11-15-1926
The resignation of Mayor A. J. Davis offered November 12, 1926 was
accepted.

5-03-1927
MAYOR: J. A. Yarborough
BOARD OF COMMISSIONERS: F. W. Dickson, W. R. Powell, R. W.
Wilkinson, E. W. Timberlake Jr., S. P. Holding

6-03-1927
The resignation of Commissioner E. W. Timberlake Jr. offered June 2, 1927
was accepted.

7-11-1927
J. C. Caddell Jr., was declared elected to fill the vacancy of Commissioner
E. W. Timberlake Jr.

11-15-1927
Dr. S. P. Holding was elected to succeed Dr. J. A. Yarborough as mayor. Mr.
G. H. Greason was elected to succeed Dr. Holding as commissioner.

5-07-1929
MAYOR: A. J. Davis
BOARD OF COMMISSIONERS: F. W. Dickson, J. H. Gorrell, R. W. Wilkinson, W. R. Powell, G. H. Greason

5-05-1931
MAYOR: A. J. Davis
BOARD OF COMMISSIONERS: S. W. Brewer, F. W. Dickson, J. H. Gorrell, G. H. Greason, W. R. Powell

7-02-1931
The resignation of W. R. Powell as town commissioner was submitted to the board and the board accepts his resignation. By unanimous vote P. H. Wilson was chosen a member of the Board of Commissioners in place of W. R. Powell.

3-03-1932
The resignation of Commissioner P. H. Wilson offered February 11, 1932 was accepted. By unanimous vote Prof. E. W. Timberlake Jr. was elected a member of the Town Board to succeed P. H. Wilson.

5-02-1933
MAYOR: A. J. Davis
BOARD OF COMMISSIONERS: S. W. Brewer, F. W. Dickson, J. H. Gorrell, G. H. Greason, E. W. Timberlake Jr.

5-07-1935
MAYOR: S. W. Brewer
BOARD OF COMMISSIONERS: Harvey Holding, Don P. Johnston, G. W. Paschal, Clyde H. Coppedge Sr., C. S. Black

2-06-1936
The resignation of Commissioner C. H. Coppedge Sr., offered February 6, 1936, was accepted. Mr. H. L. Miller was elected commissioner to fill unexpired term of C. H. Coppedge Sr.

5-04-1937
MAYOR: A. J. Davis
BOARD OF COMMISSIONERS: G. W. Paschal, Harvey Holding, Don P. Johnston, C. S. Black, R. L. Harris

5-02-1939
MAYOR: Harvey Holding
BOARD OF COMMISSIONERS: G. W. Paschal, R. L. Harris, C. S. Black, W. D. Holliday, Sam Sidenberg

5-06-1941
MAYOR: Harvey Holding
BOARD OF COMMISSIONERS: B. H. Hobgood, C. S. Black, W. D. Holliday, Sam Sidenburg, O. C. Bradbury

9-25-1942
Dr. C. S. Black's resignation is accepted by unanimous vote. Mr. J. W. Hollowell was elected commissioner to fill unexpired term of Dr. C. S. Black.

5-04-1943
MAYOR: Harvey Holding
BOARD OF COMMISSIONERS: O. C. Bradbury, B. H. Hobgood, F. M. Beddingfield, I. B. Lake, W. D. Holliday

5-08-1945
MAYOR: Harvey Holding
BOARD OF COMMISSIONERS: O. C. Bradbury, B. H. Hobgood, J. A. Easley, C. S. Black, J. M. Brewer

5-06-1947
MAYOR: W. L. Royall
BOARD OF COMMISSIONERS: J. M. Brewer, B. H. Hobgood, C. S. Black, J. A. Easley, W. W. Holding III

6-03-1948
Mr. B. H. Hobgood tendered his resignation as a member of the board of commissioners which was accepted with regret by the board. By unanimous vote, Mr. G. V. Barbee was elected a member of the board of commissioners to fill the unexpired term of Mr. B. H. Hobgood.

2-03-1949
W. W. Holding III tendered his resignation as a member of the Board of Commissioners because he was moving out of town. This resignation was accepted with regret. By unanimous vote, Dr. O. C. Bradbury was nominated to fill out the unexpired term of W. W. Holding III, as a member of the Board of Commissioners.

5-03-1949
MAYOR: W. L. Royall
BOARD OF COMMISSIONERS: C. S. Black, A. L. Aycock, C. B. Sabiston, G. V. Barbee, J. E. Wooten Jr.

5-08-1951
MAYOR: W. L. Royall
BOARD OF COMMISSIONERS: A. L. Aycock, G. V. Barbee, C. S. Black, C. B. Sabiston, J. N. Bond

5-01-1952
Commissioner Bond tendered his resignation from the board which was accepted with regret. By unanimous vote, Mr. J. E. Wooten Jr. was elected a town commissioner to fill the unexpired term of J. Nurney Bond, resigned.

1-01-1953
Mr. G. V. Barbee tendered his resignation as a member of the Board of Commissioners which was accepted with regret.

2-05-1953
By unanimous vote, Mr. John B. Cole was elected town commissioner to fill the unexpired term of G. V. Barbee, resigned.

5-05-1953
MAYOR: H. L. Miller
BOARD OF COMMISSIONERS: A. L. Aycock, C. S. Black, J. N. Bond, John B. Cole, W. H. Holding

5-03-1955
MAYOR: H. L. Miller
BOARD OF COMMISSIONERS: W. H. Holding, John B. Cole, J. N. Bond, J. E. Anderson, John T. Wayland

8-02-1956
Commissioner Bond tenders his resignation as a town commissioner in that he will no longer be a resident of the Town of Wake Forest. Motion by Commissioner Holding that the board accept the resignation, seconded by Commissioner Cole, and carried by unanimous vote. By unanimous vote, Nash H. Underwood was elected a town commissioner to fill the unexpired term of J. N. Bond.

5-07-1957
MAYOR: H. L. Miller
BOARD OF COMMISSIONERS: W. H. Holding, Nash H. Underwood, John T. Wayland, John B. Cole, J. E. Anderson

5-05-1959
MAYOR: Ben T. Aycock
BOARD OF COMMISSIONERS: Stewart A. Newman, John T. Wayland, W. H. Holding, Nash H. Underwood, Paul K. Brixhoff

5-02-1961
BOARD OF COMMISSIONERS: John B. Cole, Mrs. Fred Harper

4-11-1963
By unanimous vote the board accepts the resignation of Mayor Ben T. Aycock. By unanimous vote, Commissioner Holding was appointed to fill the unexpired term of Mayor Aycock.

05-07-1963
MAYOR: S. W. Brewer Jr.
BOARD OF COMMISSIONERS: W. H. Holding, Nash H. Underwood, Paul Brixhoff

5-04-1965
BOARD OF COMMISSIONERS: John B. Cole, Mrs. Fred Harper

5-02-1967
MAYOR: Paul Brixhoff
BOARD OF COMMISSIONERS: Thomas J. Byrne, Walter H. Holding, John Lyon

5-06-1969
BOARD OF COMMISSIONERS: Mrs. Dessie W. Harper, J. Carroll Trotter

5-04-1971
MAYOR: John D. Lyon
BOARD OF COMMISSIONERS: Tommy Byrne, John B. Cole, Ailey M. Young

11-04-1975
MAYOR: Thomas J. Byrne Sr.
BOARD OF COMMISSIONERS: John B. Cole, Guy G. Hill, Ailey M. Young

11-6-1979
MAYOR: James A. Perry Jr.
BOARD OF COMMISSIONERS: Terry W. Carter, Lyman C. Franklin, Guy G. Hill

12-17-1981
BOARD OF COMMISSIONERS: Ms. Kenille Prosser, Mr. Fred Chandley

11-8-1983
MAYOR: Thomas J. Byrne
BOARD OF COMMISSIONERS: Rodney V. Byard, Alphonza C. Merritt, John F. Sanderford

11-6-1985
BOARD OF COMMISSIONERS: William Edwin Alford, John G. Mills III

11-3-1987
MAYOR: Jimmy Ray
BOARD OF COMMISSIONERS: John F. Sanderford, Rodney V. Byard, Hope N. Newsom

11-7-1989
BOARD OF COMMISSIONERS: Edwin Alford, John G. Mills

11-5-1991
MAYOR: Jimmy Ray
BOARD OF COMMISSIONERS: Robert N. (Bob) Hill, John F. Sanderford, McLester (Mac) Turner

9-23-1992
Mayor Ray on leave of absence. Mayor pro tem Bob Hill assumes the duties of mayor until such time as Mayor Ray returns from his leave of absence.

10-08-1992
By unanimous vote, Commissioner Mills was designated "acting mayor pro tem" for the duration of Mayor Ray's leave of absence in the event of an emergency situation.

1-11-1993
Mayor pro tem Hill read a letter of resignation from Mayor Jimmy Ray. He also read the following press release:

As of 10:00 a.m. this morning Jimmy Ray has submitted his resignation as mayor of the Town of Wake Forest. It is regretful that this action has become necessary for an individual who has given so much time and effort to this community.

This brings to a close an unusual and particularly stressful period for the Town, its citizens, its elected officials and employees. It is now time for the Town Board of Commissioners to move ahead and deal with the responsibilities placed upon them by the Town Charter.

By unanimous vote, Commissioner John Mills was elected to serve as mayor .

1-11-1993
Commissioner Sanderford made a motion to nominate David Williams, seconded by Commissioner Alford. Commissioner Turner said that while he is sure Mr. Williams would make a fine board member, he was not aware of his interest until several hours ago and made a substitute motion to nominate Mr. Boyce Medlin. Commissioner Turner's motion died for lack of a second. Commissioner Sanderford's motion carried unanimously.

11-2-1993
MAYOR: Richard T. (Dick) Monteith
BOARD OF COMMISSIONERS: Joseph Cooke Jr., Richard Finke

2-22-1994
Commissioner Sanderford passed away on February 14, 1994.

3-15-1994
By a vote of three to one, Rod Byard was duly elected commissioner to be sworn in at the April 19th board meeting.

11-07-1995
BOARD OF COMMISSIONERS: Daniel R. Heimbach, Robert N. (Bob) Hill, A. S. (Al) Hinton

4-16-1996
Commissioner Joseph Cooke Jr, resigns.

5-21-1996
The vote was three to one for Velma Boyd and she was declared to be duly elected commissioner to be sworn in at a special called meeting to be held on June 4, 1996.

11-02-1993
MAYOR: George C. Mackie Jr.
BOARD OF COMMISSIONERS: Thomas G. Walters, Boyce C. Medlin

1-12-1999
Letter from A. S. (Al) Hinton resigning as commissioner at the next regularly scheduled meeting.

2-16-1999
Velma Boyd appointed to fill vacancy due to resignation of Commissioner Al Hinton.

11-02-1999
BOARD OF COMMISSIONERS: Vivian A. Jones, David K. (Kim) Marshall Sr., Velma A. Boyd

11-06-2001
MAYOR: Vivian A. Jones
BOARD OF COMMISSIONERS: Chris Malone, Rob Bridges

11-20-2001
By requirement of the North Carolina General Statute, Commissioner Jones resigns her position as commissioner on the Board of Commissioners due to being elected mayor of the Town of Wake Forest. By unanimous vote, David Camacho appointed to fill the vacant commissioner seat, which is an unexpired term ending December 2003.

2-04-2003
Approval of resignation letter from Commissioner Kim Marshall.

3-18-2003
By unanimous vote, Thomas Walters was appointed to fill the commissioner seat left vacant due to the resignation of Kim Marshall.

11-04-2003
BOARD OF COMMISSIONERS: Stephen R. Barrington, Velma Boyd, David Camacho

11-08-2005
MAYOR: Vivian A. Jones
BOARD OF COMMISSIONERS: Margaret Jones Stinnett, Dallas Franklin (Frank) Drake

11-06-2007
BOARD OF COMMISSIONERS: Christopher Kaeberlein, Peter Thibodeau, Anne Hines

index

Note: The appendix is not indexed.

about the author

Carol Pelosi and her family moved to Wake Forest in the summer of 1970 from Syracuse, New York, with a two-year stay in between in Fayetteville, Arkansas. She worked for *The Wake Weekly* for 10 years as a typesetter and reporter, moved to a local software company where she was the purchasing agent for 15 years, and returned to *The Wake Weekly* for a three-year stint as the editor. Now retired, she publishes an online weekly newspaper about the town, *The Wake Forest Gazette*.

WAKE FOREST is on the Seaboard Air Line Railroad, seventeen miles north of Raleigh, the capital of North Carolina. Including Glen Royall, the cotton mill village, it has a population of 2,500. In addition there are a thousand students of the College not counted in the census. Situated in beautifully rolling uplands, WAKE FOREST has a climate and health record unsurpassed. The mean temperature for the summer is 71.8; for the winter, 54.4.

WAKE FOREST has long been admired for its beauty. The College Campus, set with a variety of evergreens and deciduous trees, and crossed by walks bordered with roses and flowering shrubbery, is perhaps the

Administration Building, W. F. C.

finest park in the State. Faculty Avenue, leading northward from the campus, has always been regarded as one of the noble residence streets. When the National Highway was built through the town, two years ago, this street, which is 100 feet wide, was developed as a boulevard for more than a half-mile. In the center is a space eighteen feet wide, for shrubbery. On each side of this is a one-way paved driveway, also eighteen feet wide, then a space set with trees and next the sidewalk. This paved street, with its extension around the Campus and to the north and south, lies for two miles in the limits of the town.

Residential Advantages

For a person of refined taste WAKE FOREST offers a cultured community in which to live. The town has grown up around Wake Forest College and is breezy with the college atmosphere. Yet there is no exclusiveness. The professors have built their homes here and there through the town, while there are many other cultured people here in no way connected with the College. Yet the entire community profits by the College, its public lectures, the public debates of the students

Water Plant